Christmas
Antiques, Decorations
and Traditions

Christmas
Antiques, Decorations
and Traditions

Constance E. King

ANTIQUE COLLECTORS' CLUB

ISBN 1 85149 297 6

British Library Cataloguing-in-Publication Data
A catalogue record for this book is available from the British Library

Printed in England
by the Antique Collectors' Club Ltd., Woodbridge, Suffolk

Frontispiece caption:
The adoration of the shepherds. Hendrick de Clerck (c.1570-1629). Courtesy Christie's Images

Contents

The Nativity. Gospel lectionary in Latin. Illuminated manuscript on vellum. Southern Germany or Bohemia, c.1500.

Acknowledgements

I first began working on the theme of Christmas some fifteen years ago and began taking photographs of interesting pieces. Through the years, I have talked to dozens of collectors in Britain and America, who are fascinated by the vast assortment of manufactured decorations, as well as individuals who remembered incidents from their family celebrations. Though not known by name, I would like to acknowledge their contribution and that of many antique dealers who have shown me interesting items. I would especially like to thank Angela Owen, who allowed me to photograph many items from her collection and Camilla Young of Christies Images, who searched out photographs of items sold by Christies in London and New York. Leigh Gotch of Bonhams Chelsea has been generous with interesting photographs. Sotheby's Billingshurst also supplied several illustrations and I would also like to thank The National Museum of Wales. Most of the collectable pieces were photographed by my husband Andrew, working through Jane Vandell Associates, and I also acknowledge his help. Unless otherwise stated, all the illustrations in this book are reproduced courtesy of the Constance King Collection.

CHAPTER I
Gather in the Holly

'Now with bright holly all your temples strow
With laurel green and sacred mistletoe'
John Gay, 1716.

The Yule log is one of the earliest surviving traditions and, by the 19th century, was often shown in conjunction with a robin. This German-made bonbonnière is constructed of carton, c.1910. Ht. 4 ¾in (12.1cm)

Christmas, a word so illuminated and wrapped around with rich sounds, scents and images that it conjures up not only a festival in the Christian calendar but an attitude of mind, a feast of pleasure, a time for both giving and receiving its bounty. Christmas brings hope in the longest nights of the year, light and colour in the darkest days, fear to people who disturb its ghosts and delight to children who explore its mysteries and store up memories for the future.

Christmas is a time of strange contradictions: an innocent baby, worshipped by wise men: a saint who both punishes and rewards : cruel pagan rites combined with sentimentality: prayer before feasting: simple traditions set against national celebrations. Christmas has survived many attempts to destroy it, has overcome rationalists, agnostics, the extremes of Protestantism and is even weathering the consumerism and selfishness of the world today. Christmas is criticised by

Right: A rare lead robin perched on holly, with a sign 'Merry Christmas'. Presumably intended as a table decoration. English, c.1910. Ht. 2 ½in (6.4cm)

Samplers of Christmas carols are unusual. This was worked by 'Elizabeth Thomas aged 14 years 6th of July 1812'. It shows the 'Song of the Angels at the Nativity of our Blessed Saviour', with verses of 'While shepherds watched their flocks by night'. 19in (48.3cm) x 15in (38.1cm).

Kate Greenaway style figures in fur-trimmed clothes from a late 19th century card album, c.1895.

successive generations for losing its old meaning but remains a feast of the senses and a time of joy and reflection in homes across the world.

The Yuletide festival has survived because of its ability to change and adapt to different cultures, without losing its essential message, that mankind was given a precious gift for good. Though interpreted in different ways and even adopted in Oriental countries because of its alluring spectacle, Christmas has endured the centuries because it offers hope for the future in a

world that people have always perceived as threatened by the forces of darkness and despair.

As a guard against these brooding evils, evergreens were carried into the houses and temples, where, according to traditions lost in the mists of time, their presence could protect against fire and lightning and the ever-present evil eye, which could ruin crops or strike down apparently healthy animals. In all civilisations, there are celebrations, sacrifices and rituals to mark the seasons of the year: the bounty of a good harvest: the fear of the cold of winter, whose ice seemed to kill all life.

In the temples of Greece and Rome, evergreen garlands and branches were tokens of propitiation to the gods. Saturn, the god of agriculture, was feted in December by a great festival, the Saturnalia, a celebration of the sun's re-birth. This was a time for dressing up, feasting and spending with a reckless extravagance unknown during the rest of the

'Winter Amusements' in the 1840s from a contemporary children's book. Published by Dean and Co. Lithographers. Threadneedle Street, c.1840.

Wassail was carried around the room or from house to house in simple carved bowls, as well as large ornamental pieces. Made of lignum vitae, a late 17th century example, with two reeded bands on a waisted socle, the cover with a ball finial. Made by a craftsman woodturner, it would attract collectors of English folk art.   Courtesy Sotheby's West Sussex

11

The hearth spirit, who inspired the burning of the Yule Log, still lurks in every chimney and mingles with the legend of St. Nicholas. Christmas card postmarked 1914.

Part child, part angel, this girl delivering toys merges with the snow-covered Christmas tree. Published by Stewart and Woolf. Postmarked 1905.

year. Across the Roman Empire, the dancing, lighting of candles and exchanging of gifts broke the silence of the winter months and provided an excuse for the reversal of all the rules of daily life. Slaves were served by their masters, there were no heavy punishments and even the children's lessons were forgotten. The Emperor Caligula inaugurated an extra 'Day of Youth', which was devoted to sports, so that the festival was

gradually expanded into a whole seven days of rejoicing. The celebration of the Winter Solstice developed very gradually into a week-long holiday for rich and poor, with an underlying message of peace and goodwill, set against cruel sacrifices and drunken licence.

The Emperor Aurelian, in 274 AD, chose 25 December, an ancient sacred day, as Dies Natalis

Invicti Solis (The Birthday of the Unconquered Sun). It was a date already celebrated as a festival of Mithras, with all the pagan rituals of evergreens and the ceremonial lighting of fires. The necessity of keeping a fire alight throughout the festival made the use of large, slow-burning logs essential and the great Yule log was surrounded by myths and superstitions. The original meaning of the word "Yule" is lost, though the strongest theory is that it evolved from an old Norse word for feasting or revelry. In ancient times, a great log was cut with rejoicing and then carried home with the ceremony demanded of a symbol whose preserved ashes could cure the sick, be used as a balm for wounds and a protection against evil.

Some of the stories connected to the Yule log must have terrified the people who clustered about it for warmth and tended it with care, so that it would smoulder through the whole festival. One tradition tells how, at the year's end, the dead returned to their hearths and required a friendly welcome. This fear of the anger of ancestors and unknown spirits forced superstitious country people to leave the ashes undisturbed as, if they were swept or troubled, the ancestors themselves would be consumed by the fires of damnation.

While the Yule log was accorded many ceremonies in Britain, it was of even greater significance in France, where, in some regions, the unburned heart of the log,

'While you lie in peaceful slumber / May he not mistake the number'. The Saturnalian evergreens associated with the old celebration of Christmas mix with the newer children's festival on an early 20th century postcard.

Christmas garlands had become more elegant by 1920, with candles, associated with ancient celebrations, combined with fir. The Father Christmas doll takes its place among toys rather than decorations, c.1920.

13

if used as part of a new plough, would have magical power to quicken the soil and ensure an abundant harvest. In Provence, well into the nineteenth century, the strong men of the family carried the log three times around the supper table before it was laid on the hearth and a generous libation poured over it by the eldest person in the room. This ceremony, with hundreds of local variations, was repeated across Europe and was a means of asking the old gods for their help in the new year.

The early church took over a few of the traditions of the Yule log, but with obvious reservations, as these rituals were unashamedly pagan. The Church decided that ash should be used, because the Infant Jesus was warmed and washed by a fire the shepherds had made of this wood. The rituals of lighting the Yule log were carried to America by the first European settlers, who repeated the old folk songs and sayings that accompanied the libation. Each community, and even individual families, interpreted this most ancient ritual of the Winter Solstice in different ways, with some in France selecting the eldest son to strike the first blow to a living tree, which had to be of a fruit-bearing variety, such as an olive: that would help the women of the family to conceive. To last for several days, the log had to be about five feet long and of substantial girth and it is probable that in the medieval period they would have been banked down with ashes at night and fanned back into flame when the next evening's celebrations began. In vast baronial fireplaces, large sections of tree trunk, supported by massive iron dogs, would have smouldered for several days but in most country houses the log would have only burned on Christmas Day. In the Deep South of America, the slaves were given a rest from labour while the Christmas log kept burning, so it was frequently damped down to extend the holiday.

Above: 'Bringing in the Yule Log' became a ritual that was celebrated in different ways in Europe and America. Idealised versions of the country house Christmas encouraged the middle classes to revive and adapt attractive customs. From a *Victorian Book of Days*, c.1880.

Above centre: 'The Lord of Misrule', who orchestrated the medieval celebration of Christmas, was a combination of a Fool and a Master of Ceremonies. From a *Victorian Book of Days*, c.1880.

Above right: 'The Mummers', in grotesque costumes, called on rich people for gifts of money in the days before Christmas. From a *Victorian Book of Days*, c.1880.

Above: 'Robin at his own burn-side with his little wee wife the wren' from *Robin's Christmas Song* by Robert Burns, c.1880.

Above left: Robin arrives to wish the King 'Merry Christmas' and, in return, is given 'The wee little wren' to be his wife. The holly device on the window would have brought good fortune. From Burns' *Robin's Christmas Song*, c.1880.

Little Jack Horner's Picture Book was a Christmas edition and the cover is decorated with garlands of holly. Jack Horner is shown 'eating his Christmas pie', c.1880. The rhyme was a reference to the distribution of lands after the dissolution of the monasteries by Henry VIII.

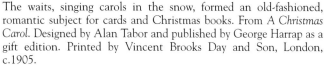

The waits, singing carols in the snow, formed an old-fashioned, romantic subject for cards and Christmas books. From *A Christmas Carol*. Designed by Alan Tabor and published by George Harrap as a gift edition. Printed by Vincent Brooks Day and Son, London, c.1905.

'The Ghost of Christmas Present', surrounded by extravagant foods. From the 1905 gift edition of *A Christmas Carol*.

By the late nineteenth century, the Yule log had become a mere token of the rituals of our pagan ancestors and perpetuated on greetings cards and in the pages of romantic novels. Made in bisque, or cheap plaster of Paris, it was found as part of the snow scene on Christmas cakes or acting as a perch for that special bird of Christmas, the robin. The cylindrical shape of the log converted easily into various types of container, inspiring the French and German fancy goods trade to produce gift boxes of card and papier mâché, ornamented with moss, flowers, or the crossed ribbons that were used in France to decorate real Yule logs.

For the few people who still have large open grates, the libation to the old gods who sleep in the log is more likely to be a light sprinkling of brandy than the brimming goblets of old, and the need for an ornamental log has to be satisfied by a chocolate roll, smothered in icing and dusted with sugar to represent snow.

The robin, who always sits on the top of the Christmas log, is another survivor from medieval Europe. The bird was regarded with awe, as it was

Charles Dickens' *A Christmas Carol* was essential reading in most homes by 1900 with many luxury gift editions printed on expensive paper.

The theme of light and darkness characterises many aspects of Christmas and perhaps explains the popularity of black children playing in the snow and making snowmen. Christmas card, c.1890.

Delivering gifts, these well-dressed children in the snow set the unattainable standards that epitomise German Christmas popular art, c.1885.

Holly decorated cards reminded the Victorians of the ancient traditions of the season. 'Christ's thorn' was also liked because of its magical associations.

Right: A winter skating scene, framed in a border of evergreens. Some scrap books were arranged with imaginative care, which makes them especially collectable. The book is inscribed 'Gilbert L. Bridgeland. 1892'.

The delights of winter in Germany were known to people across the world because of the huge export of chromolithographed scraps, often showing skating scenes, c.1875.

Holly and mistletoe, the perpetual symbols of Christmas, with their origins in the old Saturnalian celebrations, c.1905.

believed to have first carried fire, which singed its breast, to earth, so that from ancient times the burning log and the robin were connected. The robin is also linked to the wren, as in the old verse 'The robin and the wren/ Are God's cock and hen' and with another myth concerning the bringing of fire, in which the wren started carrying the flame to earth, but the robin took over, again burning its breast. More directly associated with Christianity, the robin was said to have plucked a thorn from Christ's crown, accidentally pricking its breast and staining it forever. Superstitions abounded concerning the danger, ill luck or even death which would result if these birds were killed. In Wales, a captured wren was carried around at Christmas in a small, ornamented Wren House, with singing and seasonal drinking and revelry. The ceremonies of the Wren House differed in various areas, but it was usually connected with the drinking of wassail. In Ireland, on St. Stephen's Day, there was a Wren Boys Procession, with the usual noisy group of young men singing and asking for hospitality. Instead of a Wren House, they carried a holly bush on top of a pole, presumably representing a bower where once a wren was imprisoned. In some of the songs connected with the wren ceremony, it seems the bird was cooked and eaten but in later survivals of this pagan tradition, the bird was hopefully set free.

Like Robin Redbreast, the mistletoe trails an aura of pagan rites and beliefs and, as all the best features of Christmas, has good and evil associations. It is thought to be the Golden Bough that Aeneas picked at the Gate of the Underworld and, when grown on oak trees, which is very rare, was revered by the Druids, who cut it only with golden sickles and allowed it to fall, untouched by human hands, into their robes. Because of its pagan associations, the plant was distrusted by the Christian church and it was not used for their seasonal decoration, perhaps because Baldur, the Norse God of Light, was killed by a dart of mistletoe, thrown by the blind god Hoder, who was urged on by Loki, the God of Evil and wept back to life by his mother, whose tears are represented by the milky berries. A Breton tradition tells that the mistletoe was once a tree, but its wood was used for the crucifixion: in shame, the great tree shrank to a small parasitical bush, though its fruit and branches still hold powers as a guard against evil.

Because, like holly, mistletoe fruits in winter, both evergreens were respected as symbols of the victory of life over the cruel elements. The cream mistletoe berries were used medicinally in many ways: as a remedy for snakebites, for toothache and for epilepsy. A cutting hung in a baby's cradle would keep a child safe from changeling fairies and preserve the family line. In Britain, the plant has pagan sexual associations and the old kissing bough, or kissing bunch, has an ancient history. The structures were made by fixing the mistletoe to a framework of bent wood or wire and incorporating apples and sometimes candles. Kissing boughs were also popular in Germany, though it was only in Britain that even the smallest twig, hidden over a door or beam, was deemed sufficient excuse for a stolen kiss.

Henry Mayhew, that indefatigable reporter of London life, commented in the 1850s that mistletoe was much less in demand than in earlier times and that in many homes 'Holly is now used instead of the true plant for the ancient ceremonies and

An idealised interpretation of the Christmas waits, usually plainly dressed workmen. Dressed in snow-suits, the children reveal how the old traditions were sentimentalised in the late 19th century. German. Ht. 6in (15.2cm).

privileges observed under the mistletoe bough'. A seller of evergreens added that mistletoe was now used 'mainly by people giving parties' and that it was purchased by the male servants. In the weeks before Christmas, the city costermongers decked their carts with evergreens and, led by a fiddler or a drummer, carried the greenery along the streets with the old cry 'Holly! Green Holly!' mixing with other traditional calls.

Despite its cruel thorns, holly, or Christ-thorn, was always considered a holy plant and suitable for churches, whereas ivy was a plant for the alehouse or tavern. The sharp thorns were seen as a protection against witches and the forces of evil and holly was, consequently, welcomed by the Christian church. In 1598, John Stow wrote that 'At the time of Christmas, every man's house, as also their parish churches, were decked with holme, ivie, bays and other evergreens'. Because witches were afraid of the power of holly, it became customary for a few leaves to be saved from the household decorations, to carry good fortune into the next year. Despite its association with taverns, ivy was equally efficacious against witches and it was frequently allowed to grow unhindered over cottages in case evil spirits were abroad.

Virtually every evergreen plant was used in the nineteenth century for decorating houses and public buildings, including yew and bay. For domestic use, ivy chains were made by threading the stem of one leaf into the point of another and forming a loop at the back – such chains were favourites for the dinner table, as the leaves shone richly against the white cloths. Despite the problems of handling 'Christ's Thorn', the leaves were stripped individually and sewn on to strips of paper or linen, to write greetings that could be pinned to the walls. These mottoes were especially liked in the 1860s, when some were made by creating individual letters out of wire, to which holly was sewn, so that 'Merry Christmas' could be written in evergreens. One writer in a ladies' magazine of the period remarked 'There is nothing that bends to the shape of letters as well as

Polly Pratt's Christmas Caller
By Sheila Young

The concept of a family Christmas was fostered by women's magazines. The December editions reveal the changing styles of celebration. Polly Pratt appeared in the 1922 edition of *Good Housekeeping*.

crinoline wires'. The same writer suggested that rose-hips could be sewn to the holly if the berries were scarce that year. For the dining room, a Moss Mound was recommended, with holly leaves decorating the surface. 'On the top, place a figure of Old Father Christmas, which may be bought at any bazaar or sugar plum shop and, instead of the holly sprig he usually holds in his hand, place a sprig of mistletoe.'

In the first half of the nineteenth century, most parish churches were profusely decorated with

Produced at the Ewenny pottery in South Wales, this wassail bowl has a complex cover decorated with loops, animals and birds. The bowl is incised 'Thomus Arthyr Maker Dec 30 1834'. Ht. 12in (35.6cm).
Courtesy Museum of Welsh Life, St. Fagan's

evergreens, but this was dying out by the 1850s. Mayhew describes the churches of old with their aisles like 'pretty shady walks' and with each pew a virtual arbour. Leaves and fruits of all kinds were utilised for decoration, though in every scheme the holly and ivy had to predominate. At Cliveden, home of the Astors, the banisters were festooned with garlands of box, yew, bay, holly and ivy, as well as other evergreens. It was always the head gardener's task to decorate the giant Christmas tree, that stood at the foot of the oak staircase and he would be formally assisted by the housekeeper, who passed him each bauble and piece of tinsel individually.

Artificial and natural evergreens, fruits and flowers were often combined by the end of the century to create a more luxurious effect. The green garlands, hung from the gaseliers or electroliers, were looped into corners, or carried across the room in swags. These inevitably heavy decorations were made by tying the greenery to ropes with string or florists' wire and then adding glass or china holly berries or silk Christmas roses. In some cottages, the holly leaves were strung on cord, one flat against the other, forming a very solid, and decidedly dangerous, prickly rope.

The revival of Christmas, which commentators believed was flagging in the 1850s, was in large part due to the girls' and ladies' magazines, which became

A certain way to every dog lover's heart, a painting of a favourite pet surrounded by holly and mistletoe, the emblems of Christmas. Painted in the 1880s by Eben H. Murray.

cheap enough in the 1870s for everyone to read. These publications popularised old traditions and advised on how to structure garlands and 'devices', such as crowns and shield shapes, which were built over wooden frames. The concept of Victorian ladies being gentle but useless ornaments is dispelled by the instructions, which expected them to handle a variety of tools, as well as to fix the heavy decorations to the walls. Dainty pursuits were not completely forgotten and a 1919 magazine suggests that Christmas mottoes could be written on a white banner by laboriously sewing individual box leaves on to a traced pattern.

The stringing of holly, rowan, or cranberries in America, was a task relegated to the children of the family, who enjoyed trailing the bead-like strings over the Christmas tree or around the festive table. In the 1860s, the family of the Oatlands mansion in Virginia decorated their home with crowfoot and laurel, as well as colourful berries. The pine branches and mistletoe were always brought in last and the decorating begun on Christmas Eve. As 80% of the people in Colonial America were of British origin, it is little wonder that the earliest traditions replicated those of the mother country or adapted some aspects of folk traditions to suit their very different life-style. It seems that the first settlers in Plymouth colony were eager to excuse

The mid-19th century was characterised by some particularly hard winters with heavy snowfalls. The Village Snowman by Wilhelm Alexander Meyerhem (1815-1882).

themselves from work in 1620, claiming that it was against their consciences to toil on Christmas Day. Though the governor at first accepted their reason, he later discovered them playing games in the street and ordered them back to work: his conscience would be offended if they played while others laboured. This conflict between the Puritanism of the colonists of British ancestry and the more relaxed attitudes of the Catholics led to very different approaches to Christmas. Cotton Mather, in his Christmas Day sermon in Boston in 1712, asked 'Can you in your conscience think that our Holy Saviour is honoured by

mirth, by long eating, by hard drinking, by lewd gaming, by a Mass fit for none but a Bacchus?' These attitudes made many of the old pagan traditions carried into the Americas from Europe wither and, by the early nineteenth century, there was little present-giving amongst families, though hymns and carols were sung and the Catholics decorated their churches and homes with evergreens. The country that now most enjoys Christmas tried to ban it in 1659, when the General Court of Massachusetts decreed that "Anyone who is found observing by abstinence from labour, feasting or any other way any such day as Christmas Day shall pay

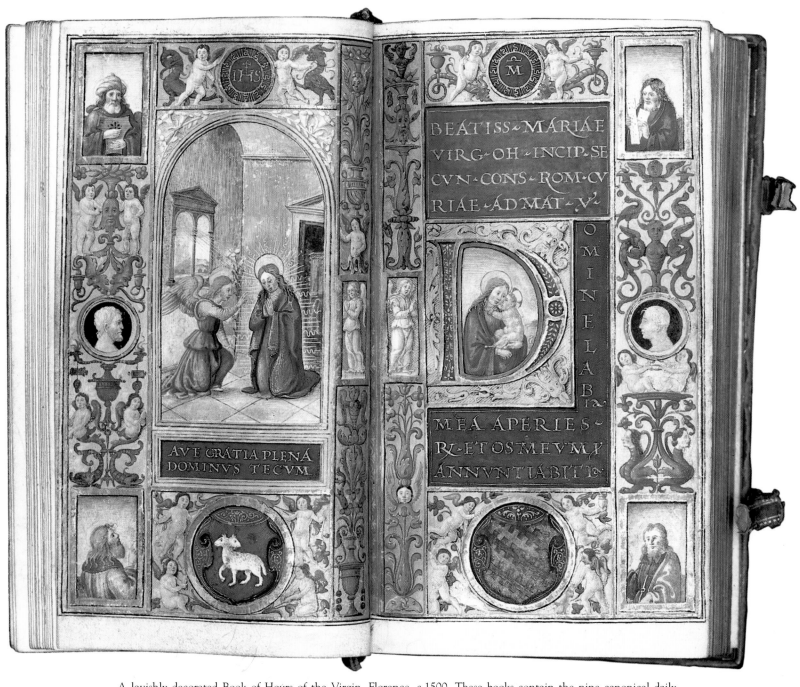

A lavishly decorated Book of Hours of the Virgin. Florence, c.1500. These books contain the nine canonical daily services, or hours. Those produced for rich patrons were colourfully illustrated with scenes of contemporary life as well as incidents from the New Testament.

Courtesy Christie's Images

for every such offence five shillings'. Fortunately, the law did not remain in place for long, presumably because it was almost impossible to enforce, and it was repealed twenty-two years later. It fell to the state of Alabama in 1836 first to recognise Christmas Day as a public holiday. Some states were slow to follow, as they were mainly inhabited by Baptists, Quakers or Presbyterians, but the pleasure people took in the celebration was irrepressible and, by 1890, the very last state to hold out, Oklahoma, accepted the legality of Christmas as a holiday.

Though the French around New Orleans had introduced many pagan customs associated with the Yule log and the Scandinavians had begun to decorate their doors with wreaths of evergreen from around 1660, American celebrations of Christmas were not memorable before 1850, except in families with German ancestors, or towns with a strong German presence.

In Britain evergreens were usually taken down and burned by Twelfth Night, but in some areas, such as Shropshire, and of course in churches, these decorations could be left until Candlemas, the Eve of the Purification of the Blessed Virgin Mary, on 2nd February. Every part of Europe had its own superstitions about the healing qualities of the ashes of the Yule log, or the protective powers of a few sprigs of holly left over from the Christmas celebrations, when all living green plants could find a place in the home. During the fifteenth century, a whole group of evergreens, including holly, holm (a form of evergreen oak similar to holly), ivy and bay were combined to create a tree in Cornhill in London, while in a pageant at Richmond for Henry VIII a tree of gold was erected with 'branches and boughs fringed with gold, spreading on every side, with roses and pomegranates, when it was drawn back the wassail or bauket was brought in and so brake up Christmas'. This extravagant and indulgent medieval style Christmas celebration ended in Britain when Charles I was executed in 1649 and the Puritans ruled. In the Act of 1652, Christmas and all its foolish revelry and superstitions were abolished. 'No observation shall be had of the five and twentieth day of December, commonly called Christmas Day, nor any solemnity used or exercised in churches'. It was eight years before this law, which was frequently but secretly broken, disappeared with the restoration of Charles II, though after this time there was a gradual decline in the Saturnalian-inspired celebration and more emphasis upon the Christian. Despite the efforts of the Protestant church to discourage ancient superstitions, they were to linger on in folk memory and even in 1906 cottagers often laid sprigs of holly on the dresser or tied them to a nail by the window. An elderly Shropshire woman explained that 'T'is good for the Angel of Peace to touch 'em when he enters the home of the sleeping'. The 1906 writer was told that it was an ancient belief in Shropshire that the good angels visited the homes of Christian folk and blessed the furniture and belongings of the faithful and that 'the holy ones particularly liked to touch the holly sprigs, being emblems of Christian rejoicing – a bit of green for angel hands to bless'.

CHAPTER II
The Nativity

'No fairy takes, nor witch hath power to charm
So hallowed and gracious is the time'
William Shakespeare, Hamlet

German colour printing was seen at its best when used for expensive die-cut and embossed three dimensional cards. Here, the nativity is enacted in an elegant ruin with putti and a gilt star. Unmarked, c.1885. 12 ½in (31.7cm) x15in (38.1cm).

Ancient pagan rituals and new Christian beliefs were merged when Pope Julius I (AD 337-352) decreed that the old celebration of the Birthday of the Sun should become Christmas Day and set in motion a festival and religious experience that would survive the ages. The simple story of a young woman searching at night for somewhere to rest before the birth of her child, the fatherly anxiety of her husband, the cold-hearted people who closed their doors and the nativity itself in a stable, involving people surrounded by animals, each dependent on the other. It is a story of such universality that it adapts to different cultures and each period in history. As science extends knowledge and life is controlled by the huge forces of international profit and greed, individuals are no more able to control their lives than was the young girl in

Classical ruins with a thatched stable made a more romantic scene than the authentic Bethlehem setting. This *Adoration of the Shepherds* portrays realistic characters with the angels and the Christ Child without haloes. Attributed to Giambattista Da Ponte (Bassano) (1553-1613).

Bethlehem who needed help. The old Christmas story still offers peace and hope and will continue to be re-told and celebrated as long as mysteries remain in the world and the birth of a child brings joy.

The central miracle of Christmas is how a story with so few recorded facts has grown and developed to such an extent that every Christian has a personal understanding of exactly what happened in that stable two thousand years ago. The mother, the peaceful Baby lying in a manger, the worshipping, roughly-dressed shepherds, the ox, the ass and the contrast of the gorgeously attired Wise Men – the world and its wisdom looking at something divine, past human understanding. Then came the legends and folk tales that surround the scene, the stories of how animals were given the power of speech at the hour of Christ's coming, trees bursting into bloom in the cold of winter, the prostration of the powers of darkness on Christmas Eve, an ever-growing tradition inspiring artists, poets, craftsmen and designers of each generation.

The story of the birth of Christ is told only in the New Testament books of St. Matthew and St. Luke and

With a sheaf of corn for a pillow, the Christ Child is adored by the animals, while a trio of angels hovers over the richly dressed Mary and Joseph. Circle of Giovanni Battista Caporali.

Before 1700, the costume and hairstyle of the Madonna often reflected current fashions and the contemporary ideal of feminine beauty, such as the medieval high forehead. Painted by Domenico di Michelino (1417-1491).   Courtesy Christie's Images

mother and fell down and worshipped him: and when they had opened up their treasures, they presented unto him gifts; gold, frankincense and myrrh.' In St. Luke, the angel of the Lord is named as Gabriel and we are told how he appears to Mary with the words 'Hail, thou that art highly favoured, the Lord is with thee: blessed art thou among women'. St. Luke's account of the Annunciation is much softer, more explanatory: 'For with God nothing shall be impossible.' His description of Mary also reveals her exultation in the words of the Magnificat: 'My soul shall magnify the Lord.' He also explains that Mary and Joseph had to undertake the journey to Bethlehem to be taxed:

'And so it was, that, while they were there, the days were accomplished that she should be delivered.

And she brought forth her first-born son and wrapped him in swaddling clothes and laid him in a manger; because there was no room for them in the inn.'

St. Luke's account is much more evocative than that of Matthew's and he introduces the 'shepherds abiding in the field, keeping watch over their flocks by night'. The Angel of the Lord appears before them, shining in glory, with the message that they would find the Babe, wrapped in swaddling clothes, lying in a manger.

'And suddenly there was with the angel a multitude of the heavenly host, praising God and saying,

Glory to God in the highest and on earth, peace, goodwill toward men.'

Luke makes no mention of the Wise Men, who feature so largely in most artistic representations of the story, though he does add words and scenes that are uplifting and it is his account, written some years after St. Matthew's, which has provided the inspiration for so many artists. Other events and characters were added to the central story of the Nativity over many years, the ox and the ass appearing in the eighth century in the Gospel of the Pseudo-Matthew, their presence at the birth fulfilling the prophecies of Isaiah and Habakkuk.

neither account carries very much detail. St. Matthew tells how the angel of the Lord explained to Joseph, a just man, that the child his betrothed wife carried was conceived of the Holy Ghost and should be named Jesus. 'For he shall save the people from their sins'. In Matthew, Chapter 2, we are told of the Wise Men from the East who had followed a bright light to Bethlehem at the command of Herod. 'And when they were come into the house, they saw the young child with Mary his

'Mary', made of pipeclay, dates to the early 16th century and comes from a group of figures recently discovered and including characters from the crucifixion and the nativity, c.1535. Ht. 3½in (8.9cm).   *Courtesy Nick Bird*

Catholic families in Britain often used the tableau of the Virgin and Child as devotional aids. Made of poured wax and costumed in expensive silks, gold lace, paper and spangles. c.1760. 11in (27.9cm) x 9in(22.9cm).

The names of the Magi were another later addition, as St. Matthew refers to 'wise men from the East' and makes no mention of their number or their clothes, though he does itemise the gifts, gold for kingship, frankincense for priesthood and myrrh for death. Gradually a tradition evolved that there were three kings: Melchior, who was an old man, Balthasar, a Negro and Kaspar, who was young. The fact that they disobeyed Herod and returned home by another route, to avoid revealing the whereabouts of the Holy Family, gave rise to many tales and superstitions regarding their subsequent adventures, which are usually spiced with magic or references to the occult. Baboushka, the Russian Christmas character, is doomed to search for the Christ Child for ever because she spitefully misdirected the Magi and refused to give shelter to Mary and Joseph. Even this character has a softer aspect and is said to put a gift under the pillow of the sleeping children she has looked at hopefully, to see if they could be the Infant Jesus and her wandering could be ended.

The first Christian celebration of the Feast of the Nativity was held in Rome c.350. In 380, the feast was also adopted in Constantinople and, as belief in

The Adoration of the Shepherds, with the angelic host being given as much importance as the Nativity. French, School of Annibale Carracci. 17th century.

Glass painting was a speciality of the Oberammergau craftsmen, though the technique of painting behind a print was widely imitated. In its original rosewood frame, pictures of this type included saints and many scenes from the Old Testament, c.1820.

Finely carved of marble, this South German or Italian Nativity scene plaque includes angels as well as the central figures of the Holy Family, c.1700. 5in (12.7cm) x 3in (7.6cm).
Courtesy Andrew Edwards

Christianity spread across Europe, the Council of Tours in 567 declared the twelve days of Christes Masse a festival. When St. Augustine, accompanied by forty monks, began to convert England in 597, he acted on the sound advice of Pope Gregory, who suggested that the people be allowed to keep their old temples and pagan altars, but that these should be used for Christian relics instead of sacrifices. In Germany, the celebration of Christ's Mass began in 813 and in Norway by the middle of the tenth century. Because the early church adopted many of the pagan traditions of the ancient seasonal winter festival, some of the Saturnalian ceremonies survived – decorating with evergreens, the lighting of candles, rest from labour and the reversal of rank, so that the servants became masters. The curious mixture of pagan mirth and frivolity and Christian worship, which created the modern Christmas, was begun in these early years and continued unabated until the Reformation introduced more sober and reflective styles of belief.

'Mother and Child', with its connections to fertility and ancestor worship, has inspired artists from the beginning of civilisation and this became the most universally popular scene from the life of Christ, because of its hopeful message and very

Skilfully modelled composition shepherds, made in Italy for domestic crèche settings, c.1910. Though cast in moulds, rather like Elastolin figures, separate detail was often applied for greater realism. Ht. 7in (17.8cm).

Large card scenes of this type were always expensive: some were prestige Christmas cards while others were intended as domestic cribs. Printed in Germany, c.1905. 12in (30.5cm) x12in (30.5cm).

human associations. While the common people were familiar with representations of the happening, it was given more realistic form for the first time when St. Francis of Assisi set up a tableau as part of the Christmas celebrations. St. Bonaventure, writing in the thirteenth century, recounted how St. Francis obtained permission from the Supreme Pontiff and then, spreading the ground with straw, brought an ox and an ass to stand next to a manger. Solemn masses were said at the manger and the hay from the crib was saved and, being so blessed and holy, was considered to be a remedy for sick animals. Bonaventure added that, during St. Francis' services in 1223, the wood echoed with bright lights and tuneful praises. Though there

was no image of a child in this early manger, the people believed that the Christ Child was there in person when the blessed St. Francis appeared to embrace him.

The idea of setting up a crib was developed in the Franciscan monasteries of France and gradually filtered through to local churches and, eventually, to grand houses. The Jesuits also adopted the custom of setting up crèches, an effective way of making the story live for the many unlettered people. The first reference to a sculptural crèche setting dates to c.645, though there is some tradition that this crèche was first begun nearly a century earlier. It was, after all, only a small step to create a three-dimensional model rather than a painting or wood carving. In 1344, a Dominican nun wrote of receiving a Christ Child in a cradle with four golden angels. These cradled figures of the Infant Jesus seem to predate the large crèche or presepio settings of Naples and it is possible that some of the crèches developed around these central figures, rather than being conceived as a complete tableau.

In 1478, the sculptors Pietro and Giovanni Almano were commissioned to create a crib scene for the family chapel of Jaconello Pepe at St. Giovanna Carbonara. This early presepio included trees as well as twelve sheep, two dogs, an ox and an ass. Interestingly, there were prophets and sibyls as well as angels. It is obvious that, by 1500, the presepio was already established in Italy, though sets with some type of mechanical movement seem to be of German origin.

Francesco de Medici was the recipient of a mechanical nativity scene around 1560, while Sophia of Saxony gave a mechanical scene to her husband in 1588. These are more in the nature of the mechanical devices for which Augsburg was famous, with silver figures of the Magi and the shepherds processing around the Mother and Child while music plays. These clockwork scenes, made of costly materials, were prestige gifts among princes and nobles and were probably among the first domestic types of cribs.

For poorer people, there were small pipeclay figures, such as those sold in Britain before the Reformation in 1534. They were intended mainly for domestic use and nativity scenes could be set up with all the appropriate characters. The figures were made from simple two part moulds and were probably sold uncoloured. A group of these pipeclay figures was discovered in the course of an excavation in 1998 and, though not complete, a sufficient number of the nativity characters had survived to indicate that complete sets were sold. There were also figures from the Crucifixion, making it obvious that their maker was producing a wider range of religious figures, though whether to be set up as shrines at home or to be offered at places of pilgrimage is debatable.

The first reference to a crib with separate articulated figures is included in a household inventory of Constanza, Duchess of Amalfi, dating to 1567. The Duchess owned a number of jointed characters, which were stored in two great chests and displayed during Christmas. Her tableau consisted of a hundred figures, including angels and animals, and sounds very much the forerunner of the vast settings which were displayed in Italy and Germany during the eighteenth century.

By 1700, the basic structure of the more expensive and detailed Italian crèche figures was established, with carved wood or terracotta used for the parts which showed, such as heads and arms, and an armature of wire, covered with tow, used for the main body. When new, the wire armature made it possible for the figures

A whole variety of genre scenes were incorporated into the Italian composition crèche settings, c.1875, which possibly inspired the simple French Santons. Ht. 4in (10.2cm).

to be bent in realistic poses, though rust now makes this impossible. In Italy, the heads were made of terracotta, with painted or inset glass eyes and skilfully modelled hair. Gradually, not just the central Christmas characters but people from all walks of life were added, so there were children, Oriental merchants, butchers and countrymen set in genre scenes alongside nobles and princes. Because the presepio figures were treasured both in great houses and in churches, their clothes have been preserved and are often of great complexity, with rich braids, fringes and expensive brocades and embroidery. As many were made in the eighteenth and early nineteenth centuries, they are the earliest antiques of Christmas that are still affordable and for many people they offer a collecting field in their own right, as fresh characters are always waiting to be discovered.

Don Carlos, King of Naples in 1734, was an obsessive collector and his presepio consisted of over 6,000 figures. Fernando IV of Naples was equally proud of his crèche and is reputed to have assisted in the making of some of the characters, while his queen and her women costumed the figures in rich silks. In Germany, the great princes and nobles were able to indulge their collecting mania with equal abandon and commissioned especially made jewellery, ceramics, turned wares and agricultural implements for their extensive and highly realistic settings. German crèche makers were more likely to work in wax or carved wood and were especially skilled in the use of perspective to create an illusion of depth and activity. Both Italian and German figures were made as portraits of actual people, so some have warts or have lost an eye or a few

The central sections of Seiffen cribs were sold complete with the Holy Family and the Magi. Additional animals and buildings carry the original prices. The card and wood building is mica decorated, c.1880. 12in (30.5cm) x 16 ½in (41.9cm).

The Oberammergau wood carvers produced the finest cribs, with finely detailed animals. This Wagnerian-style angel is fixed to the carved ruins by a wire. German, c.1890. 16in (40.6cm) x 25in (63.5cm).

teeth. As the figures were pegged in position through holes in the feet, the shoes are always substantial, even on court ladies. Angels are invariably barefoot or wear sandals, so they can easily be identified, even if their costumes are lost. The rarest have wings, but many stand or fly in attitudes of blessing and are not winged.

In eighteenth century Naples, the presepio sometimes occupied a complete floor of a large house, with merchants competing with the nobility for the most complex, artistic settings. Cows, elephants, pigs, prancing horses and monkeys were all produced for the presepio settings and are now even harder to find than the figures. Marked, fully attributable pieces are rare, though many of the artists who worked on presepios are known. A bullock at the Metropolitan Museum of Art in New York has 'Gallo' inscribed on the stomach, for Francesco Gallo, who was a modeller at the Royal Porcelain Factory in Palermo in 1788 and was known for his fine depictions of animals.

Other presepio artists worked at the Capo di Monte factory as modellers, which accounts for the superb quality of the expressive portraits. Among these were Giuseppe Sanmartino (1720-1793) and his pupils Angelo Viva, Salvatore di Franco and Giuseppe Gori.

Buildings and figures for domestic and toy crèche settings were sold in the German crib markets. Each year, new figures and buildings could be added. This classical 'ruin' has tiled floors and steps to different levels so scenes could be set out inside, c.1870. Ht. 14in (35.6cm).   Courtesy Constance King Antiques

Most of the artists worked on important sculptures for the great churches and monasteries but were also called on to design and assemble large presepio as special commissions. Court inventories list some of the work undertaken and this has enabled a few figures which were unmarked to be attributed, though in general crèche figures are valued for their artistic quality and the originality of costume, rather than maker's name.

German crèche figures contrast well with the Italian, as they were usually carved from wood and have jointed, articulated wooden bodies. As the heads were individually carved, they have more life and vigour than the terracottas, which were moulded. In some instances, inset glass eyes and wigs were used, though carved hair is found on the finest examples. The large foreground figures, such as the kings mounted on superbly carved

horses, are very rare, though examples can be seen at the Folk Museum in Oberammergau, the centre of the finest school of woodcarvers. In the Bayerisches National-museum in Munich the range of different materials that German craftsmen used in the eighteenth and early nineteenth centuries can be examined, from heavenly hosts, delicately carved in ivory, to wax settings with hundreds of individual figures.

Stables in Bethlehem at the time of the Nativity were simple caves, but the crib makers devised ruins, romantic groves, ruined temples and shell-encrusted grottoes to create their magical and impressive landscapes. Though the clothes are not such accurate miniatures of contemporary fashion as those made in Italy, they are so embroidered, sequinned and lace-encrusted that they resemble complex pieces of

Mary, Joseph and the Infant Jesus surrounded by peasants, merchants' wives and worshipping kings. Mary's dress is particularly fine and, like that of the Christ Child, is decorated with gold fringe and lace. These late 18th century Neapolitan figures have terracotta heads that are finely painted. St. Joseph is 18in (45.7cm) tall.

Set against a classical ruin and with an angel kneeling at her feet, Mary is depicted as a beautiful wealthy woman of the period. Jacopo del Sellaio (1441-1495).
Courtesy Christie's Images

characters for crèche settings, which were intended more for children, were available throughout the nineteenth century at street markets and the Christmas fairs, which were such a feature of the German Christmas. In Munich, a crib market was held in a narrow alley off a noisy main street. A reporter in a German magazine commented in 1910 that 'with the very words "crib market", the child's heart beats faster, as it is a word that unlocked all the most beautiful things man can accomplish. Blessed memories of youth…it is a time when the Munich boys and girls drag out the cribs from store and set them festively in the corner of a room. One is a ruined heathen temple with broken pillars, palm trees and cypresses…another is a plain stall made from a pair of boards, draped with pine branches…this is a joyous custom, particularly common in Catholic families in Munich.'

The children gathered in the crib market to select a new scene or to add fresh sections to one they already owned. Single pillars, walls, rocks, stars, trees of all descriptions, antique Roman and Baroque facades, all stood on tables before little old wizened wives, whose shivering fingers were blue with cold, despite their heavy clothes. Then the figures, complete regiments of wax-headed shepherds, herds of sheep, cattle and asses, the Three Kings, with every possible retinue from elephants to processing on foot with their servants, then the stags and deer which always appear in German toy cribs. The writer comments too on the boxes and chests, which contained hundreds of replacement parts: new wax heads for the main figures, wax hands and feet. 'The Christ Child in thousand-fold versions, the golden star as well. As if the whole of heaven came down to the Crib Market to be sold.'

For wealthy children and adult buyers, the crib market offered works of art from the wood-carving studios of Oberammergau and Berchtesgaden, beautifully painted and wearing expensive costumes. With them, wonderfully carved animals, prancing horses with rich trappings,

jewellery rather than people. German families still like to own a few antique figures, though most are of such high quality that they remain on display as works of art throughout the year.

Cheap carved wooden and moulded composition

Balthasar, the black King. Made of pipeclay and uncoloured, the figure comes from a group recently discovered in a London excavation. Dating to the beginning of the Reformation in England, this is one of the earliest surviving pieces made for sale to the general public, c.1535. Ht. 4in (10.2cm).
Courtesy Nick Bird

The townsman and his wife, skilfully characterised by the Neapolitan modellers, c.1780. They have terracotta heads and are costumed in the richly decorated clothes which denoted their wealth. Ht. 19in (48.3cm).

The complete Neapolitan crèche setting, including kings, peasants, merchants and their wives. The majority have terracotta heads and all are finely dressed in original costumes, c.1780.

fence. The toys could be carved or moulded in composition, were sold with or without electricity and were more expensive if a musical box playing 'Silent Night' was included. These toy cribs were made up of eleven figures and six animals and there was another, smaller set made of papier mâché. As all the figures were available separately, they could be added to or replaced as required, which is why when old cribs are discovered, they so often include figures of different materials and even different periods. Pre-1925 toy cribs in good condition are now rare, but they are liked by collectors as they are relatively small and can easily be displayed, whereas the church and princely settings need large rooms. The toy sets are fascinating, as they are sometimes made in a naïve manner, which can be as attractive as the curious animals in Noah's Arks.

As the fame and splendour of the German and Italian crèches spread across Europe, the settings began to be imitated by ordinary people, who wanted to bring the sanctity of the church cribs into their homes. The manufacture of crèche figures for a much less affluent market became a folk industry in the early seventeenth century, when religious figures began to be carved in the Tyrol. In the early eighteenth century, Johann von Metz began to organise the trade and set up distribution and collection centres, so that the woodcarvers no longer had to transport their own work across the country. Most of the men and women of the area were involved in the carving industry, though the figures were sent to special workshops for painting. The religious figures were carved of Swiss pine, but even by 1900 the wood often had to be imported because there was no policy of replanting. The most important merchants who exported carved figures for crèches across the world were Insam, Purger and Prinoth. Bohemian craftsmen were already famed as carvers of crib figures by 1800 and some carving was also undertaken in the Erzgebirge. These figures were not costumed in rich fabrics but were carved dressed and

mustard-coloured camels loaded with packages: 'there stand the little ones and look at these marvels that are, for most of them, unattainable and there creeps into the poor child's heart, perhaps for the first time, a feeling of bitter disappointment.'

German and Viennese toy catalogues of the first years of the twentieth century provide an insight into the type of setting which would have been sold in the Munich crib market. Ant. C. Niessner in 1905 offered his clients a choice of a Nativity set in a rocky landscape or one that resembled a farm with a neat

could be painted or sold plain. Waldkirchen sample books of the 1850s reveal that these traditional unpainted crèche scenes were still popular. One set contained Mary with the Infant Jesus, one angel, one shepherd, three kings and a peasant woman carrying a lantern. Joseph was not included, but there were eight sheep, a cow, a donkey and some fencing so that the scene could be contained. This type of crèche was used in particular around the base of a Christmas tree or as part of the Christmas mountain arrangements which were a special feature of the Erzgebirge region. Christmas Mountain scenes probably evolved from the great crèches and presepios seen in churches but were given regional interest by the addition of houses, vehicles and local people. In the Saxon and Bohemian parts of the upper Erzgebirge, works of art were imitated by local carvers and made small enough to be accommodated in the family home. Each generation added figures and scenes to the setting, and some became so large that eventually they took up a complete room.

Oriental merchants from a large Italian crèche setting. The figures have terracotta heads and lower limb sections and wear brightly coloured original costumes, c.1790. Ht. 10in (25.4cm).

A group of carved wooden characters from a Seiffen crib, c.1880. The chimney sweep is traditionally associated with good luck while the woodsman and the fisherman are local people. The firms which made Noah's arks also produced cribs and farms. Ht. 4in (10.2cm).

Winter sports scenes were frequently included in Christmas Mountains and American Putz. This fabric, felt and wire, fashionably dressed lady has an exceptionally well made bob-sleigh, c.1920. Ht. 5in (12.7cm).
Courtesy Constance King Antiques

Right: cribs were sold in the Christmas markets across Germany. Both buildings and figures could be purchased separately. Made in the Seiffen region, c.1880, this extensive wood, card and mirror setting includes a large flock of sheep with flowered collars. 12in (30.5cm) x 16 ½in (41.9cm).

Boxed toy Christmas Mountains were sold for children in Germany but many adults created complex mechanical versions, such as this setting including animals and trains, made over a thirty year period by Friedrich Nötzel of Brunlos in the Erzgebirge.
Courtesy Christopher P. Grauwiller

The earliest Christmas Mountains date from the 1820s and are thought to have evolved from a combination of the artistic concept of the presepios and the mechanical skills of the Erzgebirge craftsmen, who had created clockwork models of mines from the late sixteenth century. By 1910, the mountains were microcosms of everyday life in the region, with mines and working railways, which were sometimes driven by electric motors rather than the old clockwork. Essentially, the Christmas Mountain is a nineteenth century development of the earlier crèches and somewhere in every setting, under a few rocks, or in a stable, the central Nativity scene is found. Because country people derived so much pleasure from making the mountains, the genre scenes became steadily more important while, for the amusement of children, figures such as dwarves were included. Just as the Italian

nobles had competed to stage the finest presepio, the peasants of this very poor region of Germany created their own magic and invited their neighbours to see their working water wheels and flashing stars. Before the re-unification of Germany this area was in the East and, under Soviet influence, the Christmas Mountains became more secular, with Mary and Joseph banished, along with the angels, so that in some late examples, the connection with the presepio was almost lost. Several toymakers sold figures and buildings for the Christmas Mountains, which could be peopled with hundreds of figures, as well as street lamps and animals. The most curious were those made by ingenious amateurs, who linked all sorts of mechanisms together: several makers claim that they had no idea how the whole thing worked, as bits were added each year. In the early Mountains, many of the small houses,

A chromolithographed, white-robed Santa carrying a Christmas tree. He is unusual, as his robe is trimmed with brown fur. He stands in a putz-type village. c.1885. Ht. 4in (10.2cm).

churches and market buildings were lit by candles, which must have created a soft and painterly effect. A few of the more prestigious in the early twentieth century were made especially for schools or hotels by various carvers' unions, the Toy Museum at Seiffen having a good example showing people returning home from church while music plays.

Christmas Mountains were too much fun to be left in Germany when families emigrated to America and gradually a fresh form emerged, popularly known as a Putz. As with the Italian presepio, the custom developed, particularly in Pennsylvania, of visiting displays set up by neighbours and there was a lot of rivalry for the finest settings. As in the German Christmas Mountains, the scene could be set up on a series of planks or boxes, which were disguised with moss, sand, wintergreen and partridge berry, to create a landscape effect. Unlike the German Mountains, the American putz usually had a Christmas tree as the centrepiece, but in other respects, the old German traditions of candle-lit churches, railways, ponds for skating, animals and groups of people shopping or carolling were repeated, as was the practice of adding buildings each year. Because the putz can grow as required, some filled complete walls, while others are simply a small cluster of houses. Some families set the scene out on a white sheet, while others spread cotton wool over the structure. At the back, greenery is arranged to provide a landscape effect.

In Bethlehem, the Christmas city, important putz displays are staged each year and attract thousands of visitors, some of whom set up miniature versions under their own Christmas trees. As the putz are assembled in churches as well as homes, the emphasis and themes can be completely secular or traditionally religious, so that the home of Santa Claus dominates one, while the Virgin and Child, with modern people climbing to worship them, might be another. The ingenuity of the putz makers has to be admired each year and the visitors are regaled with cookies in Christmas shapes, as well as the usual alcohol. The old cookie-cutters, which were made in the past by local blacksmiths or itinerant workers, are now avidly collected, especially those that come within the realm of Christmas collectables. Early putz buildings, fences and characters figure largely in any Christmas collection, especially the buildings originally intended to be lit by candles. Water mills, churches and towers all gave the model villages more realism and were made of cardboard, wood or composition substances. The putz is such an essential feature of Christmas that complex modern versions are made, glistening with snow and ready wired so that cheerful lights can shine from the buildings clustered around the tree.

A rare German mechanical nativity scene of lithographed paper on wood. The angels fly in circles while the figures process to the sound of music. Key-wound with two carols. c.1890. Ht. 24in (61cm).   Courtesy Constance King Antiques

Peasant women carrying wood and food from a domestic crèche setting, made in Italy, c.1910. Italian makers' work is characterised by its vigour of movement and sympathetic colours. Ht. 7in (17.8cm).

Today, the putz has been adopted by families across America, who enjoy the process of setting up a new scene each year. As the concept of the Christmas landscape is universal, elements of disparate traditional crèches and presepio can be integrated, even scenes that include little Santons of French origin.

In general, French crèche figures are not as highly regarded as those of Naples and South Germany, as their modelling was not as good and the costumes were less exotic. The setting up of crèches first developed in the South of France because of the influence of the Franciscan monasteries and soon it was fashionable for them to be assembled in large houses and local churches. Unlike the German settings, the French favoured an arrangement with the Holy Family set out to one side, so that the effect was mainly that of processing worshippers. Expensive glass nativity scenes

and some white faience figures had graced the collector's cabinets of the nobility in the mid-eighteenth century and there were simpler papier mâché versions for the middle classes, but in the last years of the century a type of simple clay figure emerged, which was to become world famous as the Santon, with the first Little Saints Festival, where the figures were sold, being held in 1803.

The Santons, little saints, were originated by Jean Louis Lagnel (b.1764), who came from Marseilles. His characters were cheap versions of the white faience figures of the mid-eighteenth century, and were probably similar to the 'bread' or dough figures popular in other European countries. Lagnel realised that, to be cheap enough to sell at fairs, the figures needed to be made in plaster moulds. As in the princely crèche settings, the Holy Family soon developed an army of worshippers, including local people. The particular charm of the Santons lies in the use of various characters from Provencal life: the garlic seller, the fishermen and knife grinders and the woman carrying the traditional Christmas cake of the region. The little figures were originally unfired and painted in water or egg-based colours, so they inevitably soon broke. Because they were moulded, Santons are not easy to date, especially as they were virtually mass-produced from the earliest period, with the decorators working from top to bottom of the figures, first painting all the hair, then the faces and the eyes. This method meant that the decoration is very crude, but keen Santon collectors claim that this adds to their charm. Today, they are fired, which obviously makes them much stronger and they are made in the region of Pont-de-l'Etoile and Aubagne.

While the great German settings were imitated in France by the cheap Santons, the mechanical cribs that had absorbed the clockmakers of Augsburg were adapted and countrified for the French regions. Curious structures were built, with several floors, and

The worshipping kings from a plaster nativity scene which, like many domestic pieces, includes additional animals of different manufacture, c.1910. Ht. 5 ½ in (14cm).

figures that appeared on a kind of stage by means of clockwork mechanisms. These cribs have a charming, primitive appeal and were made in a variety of materials, from wood and wax to shells and mica. Some incorporated a coin in the slot device and were available for the public to set in motion in churches or at fairs. These rustic clockwork crèches always incorporate local characters and there is invariably a stream with fishermen. Because some of these French provincial settings are so crudely made, they were lightly regarded in the past, though their primitive, rustic effect is now popular.

Protestant churches have always regarded the setting up of crèches with suspicion, as the figures were tainted by their association with 'graven images', so the crèche never became as popular in England and America as in France or the Catholic South of Germany. In Poland, in the second half of the eighteenth century, nativity scenes were banned from churches, as they detracted from the sanctity of the services. The common people

were saddened by the loss of a spectacle they understood and began to adapt the crèche for the streets, by setting a portable version on a platform or into a type of box. Some of the Polish cribs, made of gaudy papers, card and foil, were extremely complex, with silhouettes, rosettes, mica windows and trellis work. Most were originally carried about on poles by carol singers, who vied with one another to display the most ornate models, in the form of baroque churches or Eastern temples. Occasionally, mechanical figures were included, which moved around the Holy Family. The making of these portable cribs, particularly in Cracow, became so popular that competitions were held for the finest miniature versions or the most complex with special light effects. As Poland adapted to Communism in the mid-twentieth century, the carol singing, religious element died away and the cribs became more theatrical in intention, with greater interest in the Devil than the Angel Gabriel. As the Cracow type cribs became increasingly secular, the makers concentrated

Italian craftsmen made innumerable crèche figures for the domestic and tourist trades. This group, dating to the 1930s, is unusual as the composition bases are marked with a moulded 'Como'. Ht. 3 ¾in (9.5cm).

on architecture, which could be imitated in bright foils and crepe papers and on the puppet characters which used the cribs as a stage and were activated from below with rods. Some sets of puppets included over thirty characters, while the shadow theatre cribs held many more. Polish craftsmen have a long affection for cut paperwork of all kinds and the decoration of the portable crib afforded opportunities for the most complex and colourful work. So many different papers were available by 1920 that fairy-tale buildings were made in great numbers, though they were necessarily fragile and have not survived in any great numbers. One of the finest, with towers and a cupola, can be seen in the Ethnographic Museum in Cracow.

Cut paperwork decorations have a history in Poland which began in the eighteenth century, when white paper patterns were used to decorate rooms at Easter and Christmas. The work became much more complex once a variety of coloured glacé papers appeared in the 1850s. Paper chandelier-like hangings, which characterised Polish interiors before the First World War, evolved from an earlier and much more primitive form, composed of feathers, berries, straw and wool. These often took the place of the old Yule trees, which

were hung with the trunk uppermost from the ceiling in the Holy Corner. Once coloured and crepe papers became widely available, the so-called Spider Girandoles took the place of the Yule tree. These were decorated with paper flowers, pompoms, streamers and stars, to create a riot of colour that changed its appearance each time it moved in the wind. Until 1910, the carollers who carried the Cracow-type cribs around the streets wore curiously structured hats, decorated with the type of paperwork found also on the Girandoles.

The carollers also carried stars which were set in a frame and put into motion by a simple crank mechanism. The makers of Polish stars utilised cut paperwork and the rays were decorated with paper streamers. Originally, in the star's centre, was a print or painting of the Holy Family, forming an inexpensive but effective and very portable shrine, whose design was to inspire many makers of Christmas tree stars and hangings. The history of Polish cribs illustrates how completely an authoritarian regime can fail when it attempts to destroy well-established popular customs, especially those that link religious belief with the folk art and spontaneous celebration of Christmas.

CHAPTER III
A Very German Tradition

'Worlds may wither unseen,
But the Christmas Tree is a tree of fable
A phoenix in evergreen'
C. Day Lewis

Fruits and sweetmeats piled on plates and laid out under the tree were a particularly German tradition. The girls sing a carol in the candlelight on Christmas Eve before receiving their gifts from the tree. Paul Barthel, c.1890.   Courtesy Christie's Images

Christmas, with its apparently ancient traditions and rituals, was firmly established in the imagination of the public by the 1890s. Every family believed that carols had been sung, plum pudding eaten and presents received from the dawn of time and looked back nostalgically to the Good Old Days, when coaches carried the Christmas mail and visitors arrived at the great houses laden with gifts. The one element which both British and American people accepted as a relatively modern innovation was the German Christmas Tree, which had been made welcome in homes across the world. It was generally agreed that the tree had come to England alongside other German customs introduced by Albert, the Prince Consort, a belief that, despite some contradictory evidence, is still paramount today.

Left: Victoria and Albert with their children around the largest of the Royal family's Christmas trees. This print appeared in magazines in both Europe and America and was cut out and pasted into many scrap books, c.1848.

Far left: A French tree, topped with the traditional star, mainly decorated with tinsel. A Christmas postcard dated Dec. 1908.

Because it so often snowed in Germany in December and many toys, decorations and nativity scenes originated in the south of the country, the romance of winter in a land that seemed to epitomise Christmas held great appeal. The German customs and practice of Christmas provided alluring copy for magazines and travel books and became familiar to people in all sections of society. In 1887, one writer recounted a trip to the Fatherland, to spend Christmas at a friend's castle. She travelled from the railway station in a pretty sledge of lightly carved wood. 'Its fur rugs, lined with crimson, its pair of cream coloured Russian ponies, with their harness studded with silver knobs and arches of silver bells over their heads.' The ladies in the party were given thick veils to protect their faces from the bitter chill of the air as the sledge glided with noiseless swiftness over the well-kept sledgeway… At the sound of the sleigh bells, two wolfhounds ran down the steps of the Schloss to greet their master. She tells how, in the village, a veiled woman walked up and down the streets after dark on Christmas Eve, carrying a beautiful infant in her arms to represent the Christ Child. Though this scene was memorable,

Carved wooden figures of the Christ Child were common in richer Catholic homes, as well as churches, and were placed at the foot of the tree on Christmas Eve. The hand is raised in blessing and, unusually, the original metal halo is still in place. Italian, c.1800. Ht. 8 ½in (21.6cm).

White-robed figures of Father Christmas are always popular, as they recall his saintly origins. German chromo, c.1910

With her rabbit ears fur hat, this Christkind is more child than angel. Santa has a grey fur-trimmed hat and the chromo is marked with the Royal coat of arms. By Appointment to H.M. The Queen, probably by Raphael Tuck, c.1890. Ht. 10in (25.4cm).

Christmas Eve at the Schloss was unforgettable for her.

At the sound of a bell, 'We rushed down a long corridor, being joined as we went by other members of the household and reached the room from whence a blaze of light betrayed the presence of the great tree. It was indeed a giant and formed a most imposing spectacle, as it stood, in the centre of the large room, dazzling with variegated waxen tapers, shimmering all over with ice-like crystals and decorated with gilded fruits and sweetmeats. The base was covered by a pyramid of tempting confectionery and gingerbread peculiar to the province and for which lots afterwards had to be drawn.'

The great tree was accompanied by tiny specimens which stood on small tables around the room, each laden with gifts: one tree and gift table for each member of the family and household. The English visitor received some Silesian linen, a gold brooch and a Surprise Ball, an old German custom that rewarded the industry of knitting a ball of wool by the discovery of little gifts that were threaded, the finest being hidden at the

Sledge rides across ice and snow added to the romance of Christmas for visitors to Germany in the 19th century. A Christmas card, c.1870.

A Christmas party invitation card. 'Dear little friend, will you come to my Christmas Party? I shall be so pleased to see you.' Dated Dec. 25, 1913.

centre. Her visit to the Lutheran church was awesome and she was surprised that she was instructed not to kneel. Arriving at church by sleigh, she sat with the baron and baroness in a gallery above the congregation, in a high-backed velvet chair, surmounted by the baron's coronet and with footstools embroidered to match. The service was conducted completely in black, but there was a full brass band that kept everyone awake.

This style of German Christmas held an irresistible romantic appeal: sleighs, snow and frost, decorated pine trees, delicious sweetmeats, warm furs and the joy of children at the Christ Child's coming. As people were able to travel more easily because of railways, stories of how the season was celebrated in Germany spread across the world and elements began to be incorporated in the festivities of other peoples. Fires, burning candles and decorated pine branches were a legacy from the old Saturnalian celebrations of the Winter Solstice but these customs were made more colourful by the introduction of the Paradise Tree into German mystery plays. This tree was decorated with apples and candles were lit around it, to represent God's gifts in the Garden of Eden, man's paradise. In the early sixteenth century, a gold tree that was decorated on every side with roses and pomegranates and with branches fringed with gold, was set up for Henry VIII at Richmond. There is evidence of the use of these celebratory Trees of Paradise in several European countries and, in the Imperial city of Türkheim in Alsace, the Stubenmeisters' accounts for the years 1597-1669 mention the cost of apples, hosts, pretty papers and threads, used for decorating a tree in the big merchants' hall, where a feast to celebrate Christmas was held.

The earliest account of decorated trees being used in the home dates to the seventeenth century, though even at this time some churchmen criticised their use. Writing in the 1640s, Johann Konrad Daumbauer of Strasbourg, a theologian, grumbled about the 'new practice' of celebrating Christmas, not with the Word of God, but by decorating a tree with dolls and sweets. Though pine branches and trees are usually mentioned, the Duchess of Orleans, writing in 1708, talks of decorated box. Strasbourg features in several of the early accounts of Christmas trees, one merchant in 1605 saying that those set up in the parlours of the town were decorated with paper roses and gold foil, as well as the usual sweets and host wafers. Roses are

Family photograph albums from the 1880s began to contain souvenirs of Christmas Eve. Here, a father in a middle-class home sets out toys for his children under a tall tree, c.1905.

Lavishly decorated with tinsel, this large family tree carries unwrapped gifts as well as decorations. One image from a stereo card 'I have something for you all', produced by Strohmeyer and Wyeman, © 1891 and published by Underwood and Underwood of New York, Ottawa, Toronto and Kansas.

Because trees in Germany were set up on Christmas Eve, Santa is often portrayed carrying a decorated tree along with the children's gifts. c.1890. Ht. 11in (27.9cm). *Courtesy Angela Owen*

A Happy Christmas to you

Father Christmas delivering a tree, with his basket of toys. His hood is circled with an evergreen wreath. Printed by Raphael Tuck and dated Dec. 23, 1905.

always linked with the Christmas celebrations because of their association with the Virgin Mary.

Early references to Christmas trees describe them as 'Trees of Paradise' or 'Christ-trees' but alongside the tradition of a decorated live tree or branch, another custom, of building a wooden tower on which candles could burn in tiers, was developing, both in Austria and Germany. In some regions, the Christmas Pyramids were roughly made of twigs, though most were of crossed

batons, so that the candles could stand securely on flat surfaces. Even by 1716, these were described as old fashioned and are thought to have developed from the branches that children had carried around at Christmas to ask for gifts. Gradually, the decoration of the pyramids became more ornate and the structures were wrapped with foil or hung with gilded nuts and berries. A print of the 1830s revealed a pyramid formed in the shape of a pine tree, with a candle at the end of each

Imitation trees made perfection attainable and provided a rigid support for the candles that have characterised the celebration of Christmas throughout the centuries. Published by Schwertleder and Co. Printed in Berlin.

Schwertleder and Co., whose cards were printed in Berlin, specialised in images of beautiful children. Postmarked Dec. 4, 1914, the artificial tree is decorated mainly with lametta.

branch and apples hung from the struts. As with a fir tree, the children's toys and gifts were arranged beneath the 'branches'. Some German families, especially those living in towns, seem to have grown very fond of their pyramids, which could be kept from year to year and one elderly Dresden lady complained bitterly in the 1880s because her father had always insisted on decorating a pyramid rather than a fir tree.

The pyramids made in the Erzgebirge region of Germany developed into works of art and evolved from simple crossed sticks into tiered buildings, with arches and metal railings within which well carved crèche figures could stand. Some pyramids have brass candleholders attached to each layer, while others were made completely of turned wood, to which Noah's Ark type figures were fixed in curious processions, a huge dog alongside a tiny peasant or a minute tree. The Seiffen wood-turners specialised in the manufacture of brightly coloured chandeliers and candle holders and the two skills were combined for the more complex Christmas pyramids, which are surmounted by large fans, turned by the heat of candles. Pre-1900 Christmas pyramids are now very hard to find, as they are treasured in families, but a few always left Germany through the tourist trade. They rarely appear in old toy merchants' catalogues, presumably because they were not thought to have held much appeal outside Northern Europe. The earliest pyramids were merely circles of wood without movement, but in the late nineteenth century, each layer turns gently in the candle heat.

Imitation trees were on general sale by 1865. A vast assortment of decorations was available by 1900, in glass, ceramics, composition, paper, card and wood. The German dolls were made by Armand Marseille and Heinrich Handwerck. Larger doll 36in (91.4cm).

The dual attraction of pyramids and real fir trees enchanted German children and as their families emigrated across the world, they carried their customs with them. From the sixteenth century, the German tradition of decorating a tree for Christmas was associated with Martin Luther, who is said to have been amazed at the beauty of the scenery on Christmas Eve, when he was walking under a star-lit sky and looking at the fir trees dressed in snow. On returning home, he attempted to re-create the effect by placing candles on the branches of a small tree. Because the great preacher approved of decorated trees, their use became widespread across Germany where the celebration was not reserved for the Catholic regions, as it was in parts of America.

Gradually, the fashion of decorating a tree at Christmas spread across Europe, with King George I introducing them to England around 1715. Queen Caroline, wife of George IV, set up a Christmas tree at another children's party in 1821, though this was fixed to a board and decorated with gilt almonds, oranges and other sweetmeats and beneath it was a little village with figures of people, buildings and animals. The custom was also spread by visiting merchants and court officials. According to Grenville's Diary, Princess Lieven set up a German-style Christmas tree at Penshanger in 1829. The fact that the use of Christmas trees became generally popular in America before England is often explained by the fact that the Hessian soldiers in George III's army are said to have set them up when they were fighting Washington's men, though their widespread popularity is much more likely to have originated from the large numbers of immigrant German families.

Despite these antecedents, in Britain most people believe that Christmas trees were unheard of until Prince Albert of Saxe-Coburg-Gotha married Queen Victoria in 1840 and introduced the customs of his own happy childhood to the court. An attractive print of the Royal couple with their young children, published in 1848 in the *Illustrated London News* and in America in *Godey's Ladies' Book*, was cut out and pasted into innumerable family scrapbooks across the world. The tree was, forever, Albert's gift to Britain and America, despite the fact that it was already known in each country and often described by the new breed of traveller, who used railways to reach previously faraway places.

Prints and paintings dating to the first quarter of the nineteenth century provide evidence of how the use and decoration of trees developed. In small houses, the trees were sometimes hung by their tops from a beam and this practice is shown in an 1826 print of a little child lying in bed with his ceiling tree hung with toys and animals. Though the shapes resemble conventional tree decorations, they would have been made of sugar, pastry or wax. Well-to-do families set up Christmas tables, with a tall, decorated tree as the centrepiece and smaller firs alongside. In an 1824 print of a typical scene of this kind, the large tree was circled with three rings of decreasing size fitted with candle holders so that it became a combination of a pyramid and a green, living tree. The children's toys and family gifts were set out underneath. Some of the early decorations were surprisingly large, and made of gingerbread in the form of knights and medieval ladies. Conventional dolls and toys also hung from the trees as unwrapped gifts, a tradition that only seems to have ended in the twentieth century, when colourful papers became common. The danger of hanging gifts near candles always caused concern, not just because of the risk of fire but also because of the grease that dripped over the ornaments, despite the candle holders.

William Hewitt, visiting Germany in 1842, grumbled about damage that was already being done to fir trees by townspeople, who cut tops and tore down branches. He describes trees that were available in markets, which were fixed into a thick board or block of wood and weighted with lead. On the board, small gardens

A gift box, c.1865, with the original ribbon for hanging from a Christmas tree. Because of their fragility, few early gift boxes have survived. 4in (10.2cm) x 2 ¼in (5.7cm).

were arranged, made of moss and fir, and surrounded with neat fences. In the gardens were small houses and groups of figures, the Holy Family being central, though there were also a stork, a dog and stags with gilded horns. A stag always appears among early tree decorations, as legend tells that it was the first animal to witness the birth of Christ and sped over the hills to warn the shepherds.

Hewitt describes how an angel was suspended by a wire from a branch of the tree above the garden. The Holy Family and the animals were roughly made of clay, with the stork having real tail feathers. Even in the 1840s, some German families kept their tree gardens from year to year and added to them,

Small goose feather trees were sometimes kept under glass. They were sold ready decorated and fitted with candle holders. The wooden bases were used for feather trees of all kinds. At the foot is a tiny amethyst glass Santa. The decorations are glass and thin metal. c.1900. Ht. 9 ½in (24.1cm).

Christmas trees and the subjects provide a description of the typical tree decorations of the 1840s. There were grotesque figures, people in the costumes of all nations, a student smoking, a peasant, a child on his rocking horse, Swiss and Tyrolean maidens and all kinds of animals. All these sweetmeats were beautifully modelled and gaily coloured, as were the fruits, musical instruments, thimbles and strings of sausages. In the mid-nineteenth century, all these edible decorations were left on the tree until Twelfth Night, when they were eaten.

Descriptions of German Christmas customs appeared in many traveller's guides and popular magazines before the famous print of the English Royal Family appeared in *The Illustrated London News*. The reporter described a tree set up at Windsor Castle eight feet high with six tiers of branches, each with a dozen wax candles. The sweetmeats were typical of those described by William Hewitt but the reporter also describes eggs filled with sweets which were hung from coloured ribbons. Under the tree were toys for the children. Because the German tree was decorated with sweets and gingerbread and was obviously considered almost wholly edible, it was set up and arranged by Mr. Mawdill, the Queen's confectioner.

Christmas trees were becoming an industry by the early 1850s, when one of the first entrepreneurs, Mark Carr, who worked as a woodsman in the Catskill Mountains, loaded pine trees onto a Hudson River steamer so they could be sold from the dockside in New York. Carr continued to sell Christmas trees for some thirty years, though by 1880 there were four hundred tree merchants in New York City alone. Many London shops sold trees and decorations by 1850, indicating how quickly the tradition spread. Freshwater and Co. in 1853 begged to announce that their Christmas showrooms were open with a vast variety of decorations: 'Eloa's plums, very choice; crystallised apricots and greengages'. From D. Evans in the Strand,

establishing a tradition that was continued in America in the Putz. Hewitt states that he gave minute attention to the description of the trees and their gardens so that his English readers 'may have a complete idea of it'. His own family was given the experience of a German Christmas by one of the local peasants, who not only cut down a tree for them but also spent weeks in making clay animals and figures which he dried by the kitchen stove. The English visitors' tree was decorated with 'Two chocolate coloured stags with gilded horns, silver apples, gold and silver walnuts, trumpets, harps, dames in country costumes, babies on swaddling boards and children riding on dogs. An angel with golden wings and a crown fluttered from the end of a bough.'

He describes local families who were handed a basket when they went into the baker's shop and then went around selecting what they wanted from a vast assortment of sugar and chocolate cakes and biscuits. Most of these were made for displaying on the

Spirit lacquered tinplate tree clips in rich colours held both candles and strings of beads in place. The squirrel is 2in (5.1cm) tall, c.1900.

bon-bon boxes, chandeliers, lamps and wax tapers were available for decorating trees and there were also cosques, magic flowers and holly trees.

Though trees were considered to be an innovation in Britain, the public was already seeking novelties and by 1860 the first artificial trees, of goose feathers that were stripped from the quills and wired to form branches, were introduced. These small artificial trees were used mainly on windowsills or on side tables. Swan and turkey feathers were sometimes used for the little artificial trees, which are still occasionally found complete with their decorations and preserved under glass domes. Christmas trees were said 'to stand like forests' in the town centres of Germany, crowded around by eager buyers. In Dresden, near the Bohemian Railway, trees remained on sale through the nights, with some sold ready decorated with pink and white paper roses.

Charles Dickens helped popularise Christmas celebrations in his *Sketches by Boz*, *The Pickwick Papers* and, way above all, *A Christmas Carol*. Dickens refused to accept Christmas as purely a commercial event and saw metaphors that could be applied to the state of man and to civilisation itself in the towering German Christmas tree, brilliantly lit with a multitude of little tapers. 'What do we all remember best upon the branches of the Christmas tree of our own young

Christmas days, by which we climbed to real life?' Dickens succeeded in making old inns, coaching, feasting and merriment attractive to ordinary people, who loved the humour and reality of his books, but he also made them aware of the duty they owed to others who were poorer or weaker, particularly in *A Christmas Carol*, which was read aloud in many families as part of the Christmas rituals and is so familiar that it is frequently re-told in the tableaux of department store windows today.

Christmas trees were so well established in Britain by 1860 that some writers expected the fashion to die out. Others suggested that a tree could be 'made at home for a very trifling cost'. An 1860s edition of *Cassells Home Guide* recommended that a good-sized fir tree of regular shape should be used. 'Cover this at regular intervals with gelatine lights, which are better and safer than wax tapers. These lights are like ordinary night lights, each one contained in a little cup of coloured gelatine, resembling the glass lamps used as illuminations when gas is not employed. Suspend them on wire, which will not catch fire. A little behind each light, arrange a bright tin reflector, a star or a silver coloured ball.' The decoration of the tree was to be completed with flags, bows of coloured ribbon, ornamental boxes, paper cones, lucky shoes, jockey caps and drums made of card and covered with paper and fabrics. Obviously, though

Right: Trees were often delivered by Santa in German chromos, following the tradition of setting up the tree on Christmas Eve. c.1925.

Below: Marked 'Germany B', this cast iron tree stand is painted in the traditional dark green but highlighted in gold. c.1920. Ht. 5in (12.7cm).

Christmas trees were known, many ordinary people still needed instruction on how to set them up correctly. In many country districts, holly trees or branches were used, as they were considered traditional and the shining leaves looked attractive in the firelight.

Heavy factory-made tree holders first appeared on sale in the 1860s and these made it possible to set up large trees without nailing the trunk to a block of wood or attempting to wedge the tree between bricks or stones in a large tub. Some of the earliest tree holders resemble window boxes, as they have low, pierced metal railings around the sides. In the late 1870s, stands incorporating clockwork musical boxes which played carols appeared in the most expensive shops, alongside the traditional ornamented jars and tubs, which concealed some kind of clamp. Most of the holders were sold for the German market and many of the cast iron versions have German mottoes in the design; occasionally a maker's name or initials are found. They were very popular in America, though the British seemed to prefer the hard task of balancing a tree in a tub or decorated bucket.

In the 1890s, G. Sohlke of Berlin was selling nickel tree stands, which not only played four carols, but also revolved: these were especial favourites in America. Similar ebony-stained stands with musical movement and embossed metal stands were supplied with artificial trees before the First World War, some of the trees having candleholders on each branch and large red

An impressive wrought-iron tree stand. Made in Germany, c.1910, this would have held a 12ft. (365.8cm) tree safely. Ht. 18in (45.7cm).

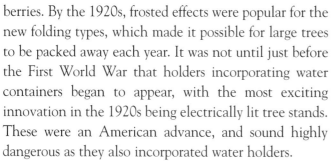

Dressing the Christmas tree became one of the traditional rituals in Britain and America by the 1870s. Though trees are always shown candle-lit in prints, they were in fact only lit for a short time because of the danger of fire. German chromo, c.1875.

berries. By the 1920s, frosted effects were popular for the new folding types, which made it possible for large trees to be packed away each year. It was not until just before the First World War that holders incorporating water containers began to appear, with the most exciting innovation in the 1920s being electrically lit tree stands. These were an American advance, and sound highly dangerous as they also incorporated water holders.

Many of these complex tree stands were only suitable for artificial trees, which were lighter, as they had wire branches. Sears Roebuck, the American mail order house, advertised artificial trees that were made in Germany in 1913. Though by this time electric lights were available, they were all sold with candle holders and bright red, sealing-wax type berries. Japanese

artificial trees were imported to America once German products became unavailable during the First World War and it was at this time that the American tree-making industry began to grow substantially.

Artificial trees reached their height of splendour in the Edwardian period, when they were made of coloured ostrich feathers and, for the most exclusive parties, festooned with velvet roses and decked with strings of artificial pearls. There was a fairly short-lived fashion around 1900 for white trees with white candles and 'angels hair' instead of ropes of beads. Such sophisticated 'adult' trees were also occasionally set up in the '20s and '30s, when silver and black was a fashionable theme. Variegated artificial trees gave further opportunities for carefully co-ordinated

A Japanese-made celluloid Santa, c.1935, with a contemporary tree. Ht. 3in (7.6cm).

St. Nicholas with his horse-drawn sleigh, laden with gifts for good children and a ready-decorated tree.

Below: Tree stands closely reflected contemporary styles. Marked 'Germany', this cast iron stand, with a metallic green finish, reveals the basic elements of the Wiener Werkstätte style, c.1925. Ht. 6in (15.2cm).

Opposite: Christmas began to be associated with Swiss holidays and winter sports in the late 19th century, when cheaper, faster travel enabled the middle classes to spend Christmas away from home. Hans Zatzka (1859-1949). *Courtesy Christie's Images*

decorations, with cellophane trees made in the '30s in New York. Curiously, though progressive materials were available, feather trees were still produced in America as late as the 1950s.

Because of the ever-present danger of fire in skyscrapers, the use of real trees and evergreens was banned in some cities, which encouraged the artificial tree and greenery makers to create large and effective displays. There was also a lot of concern over the people who plundered the forests for trees and tree tops. When Theodore Roosevelt moved into the White House in 1901, he outlawed real trees from the building and tried to persuade everyone else

to follow suit. His son secretly set up a Christmas tree in a cupboard, forcing his parents to admire his initiative and, incidentally, to re-introduce the real tree.

Very occasionally, decorated feather trees under glass domes come on to the market and there are larger versions that stand in wooden, tub-like bases decorated with painted flowers, but for most collectors the Christmas tree is celebrated by its images, either in richly coloured chromos or in prints and paintings. Embossed pressed card and papier mâché trees are occasionally discovered, as are the tree skirts which covered the stands. Commercially made versions, decorated with

printed Father Christmas figures and toys, are obviously the most popular, but there are also some charming home-made skirts, which have to be assessed by the quality of their design or some particular feature, such as an unusual fairy or other Christmas character.

Even more unusual are the Tree Carpets, which were decorated with Christmas scenes, especially Santa in his sleigh. The carpets were particularly useful when complex arrangements, such as buildings, were set up under the tree, but they were also functional in catching the pine needles. Though designated by collectors as 'carpets', they were made of a plush fabric and usually edged with a cheap cotton fringe. Prints, children's books and Christmas cards all suggest that the tree was an essential decoration in the early twentieth century, but in fact relatively few homes, it has been suggested as low as one in five in Britain, ever set one up, as the tradition was never as deeply rooted

The custom of wearing fancy dress for the Winter Solstice originated in ancient Greece. Adults and children dance in a ring around the candlelit tree. Elizabeth Adela Stanhope Forbes (1859-1912).

Courtesy Christie's Images

as in Germany. Country families who were interviewed in the early years of the century often remarked on kissing boughs, garlands of holly and sometimes a holly bush which was brought into cottages and decorated, as fir trees were commonly associated with grand houses and townspeople.

The whole concept of Christmas as we accept it today was in fact created for the growing middle classes of the mid-nineteenth century, who enjoyed filling their homes with attractive decorations and who had money to spare for pretty frivolities in glass, porcelain and papier mâché, which were only used for a few weeks of family celebration each year. In the eighteenth century, Christmas was characterised by the hospitality shown to neighbours and employees but by 1900 people had drawn in on themselves to a very much greater extent and Christmas had become an individual celebration, with families establishing their own traditions, especially those connected with the tree, the domestic centrepiece of the festival.

CHAPTER IV
Angels and Fairies

'The Angels keep their ancient places –
Turn but a stone and start a wing!
'Tis ye,'tis ye, your estranged faces
That miss the many-splendoured thing'
Francis Thompson

Crib figures, fairies and even Santas were made in this stylised cone shape in the late 1950s. This fairy, with gold paper wings and book and a plaster head, is decorated with fabric over a card core, c.1959. Ht. 5in (12.7cm).

Winged terracotta angels shed a soft but splendid glory over the grisaille shades of the Medieval Sculpture Hall each Christmas, when the Metropolitan Museum, for a brief time, becomes a shrine for the heavenly host. While European churches and museums arrange formal crèche settings, New York creates a unique blend of Christmas Tree and presepio, so lovely in its Fabergé-like detail that in its presence the most urbane fall silent. Around the foot of the thirty feet high tree are set scenes of daily life, as well as the central group of the Holy Family but, ascending all the branches, are hosts of winged angels and cherubs, all created by Italian artists in the eighteenth century and now gently illuminated by shaded lights.

Such exquisite angels were originally the province of princes and churches and formed part of formal crèche

settings, but gradually less detailed models began to be sold in the crib markets of Germany and these were hung on Christmas trees. All the early prints of German trees reveal the presence of at least one Christmas angel, though many were made of sugar or gingerbread rather than carved wood or moulded terracotta. The earliest angels produced exclusively for the domestic market are made of wax, either cast in two part moulds or constructed rather like play dolls, with fabric bodies. The carved German versions are made in the manner of the early crèche figures and some are finely painted and have gilded wings. Angels of this type were available in the crib and Christmas markets of Europe and could be bought separately to add more incidents to the family crèche or to hang on the Christmas tree each year. The finest carved figures are extremely delicate and relatively few have survived from the small cribs that were sold for family use. Wax angels led an even more hazardous existence, as many have melted or become misshapen because of the heat of the candles.

Messengers who carried the words and advice of the gods to earth were accepted by the Greeks and Romans, who invested them with wings to carry them across the heavens. Animal-like creatures, as well as figures based on the human form, were given wings, with Hermes, the divine herald, having them on his feet and headdress. Ezekiel, the prophet, c.560BC, described angels in the likeness of man, each with four faces and two pairs of wings, which were joined to those of the next angel, so they moved as a group and sparkled like burnished brass. 'The noise of their wings was like the voice of great waters, like the noise of a host.' Some angels have always been thought of as beautiful and there are many ancient tales based on the belief that angels and humans can beget children. In Judaic tradition, the angels Raphael, Gabriel, Michael and Uriel are grouped about God's throne. Gabriel, the Angel of Revelation, is made of fire and carries God's message to humans; Raphael is a seraph and an Angel of Providence, who guards humanity; Michael is Prince of the Heavenly Hosts and Uriel is the Angel of Retribution, who brings the knowledge of God to man. Despite their understanding of humans, angels, in the Christian tradition,

As much an elegant, decorative panel as a religious icon, the Pre-Raphaelite lady wears rich aesthetic dress. John Melhuish Strudwick (1849-1937).

Courtesy Christie's Images

In the New Testament, angels are associated with Christ's empty tomb and St. Peter is rescued from prison by a heavenly presence, which leads him past his guards. By the fourth century, the old classical style angels had merged with Christian concepts and they were portrayed more as protectors than avengers. Angels were popular with ordinary people, who could call on them for help, though they were periodically banished from the church as idolatry. In the Middle Ages, each month was governed by its angel, as were the four elements. Michael was said to rule the East, Gabriel the North, Raphael the West and Uriel the South. This was the period of great scholastic debates regarding the powers and composition of angels, one bishop suggesting that good angels and bad had bodies of fire and air. In the mid-thirteenth century, St. Thomas Aquinas once held fifteen lectures on angels in a week and from the work of this great scholar were derived most subsequent Catholic interpretations, which were only displaced by Protestant theology in the sixteenth century.

Though the churches of Martin Luther (1483-1546)

All the wealth and earthly weight of the costume of a Renaissance prince burdens the Angel of the Annunciation. A wing of an altarpiece triptych. South German School, c.1520.

Courtesy Christie's Images

Though low in the hierarchy of angels, cherubs could be portrayed playing, singing or sporting mischievously, like beautiful infants. Follower of B. Luini, c.1481-1532.   Courtesy Christie's Images

have no gender or substantial form, but can protect, influence and guide humanity. Because of the universal belief that the soul in some way survives death, angels are frequently associated with those spirits and by the second century AD, there was a widespread belief in guardian angels and in the concept that everyone had a good and evil presence, one sitting on each shoulder.

Some Christ Child figures are carved with an unusual degree of realism and with particular attention to the hair and hands. This Italian version wears a gold-embroidered robe. Late 18th century. Ht. 11½in (29.2cm).

Made in Germany, this waxed composition fairy in her tinselled gauze dress was made for the British market and carries a sequinned wand. She has a fabric body and waxed lower limb sections, c.1880. Ht. 14in (35.6cm).

and John Calvin (1509-1564) largely dispensed with the hierarchy of angels, they were never able completely to persuade the ordinary people to abandon their helpful friends and in the seventeenth and eighteenth centuries crèche settings, as well as prints and paintings of the Nativity, gave artists many opportunities to explore the subject. In several of the Tyrolean cribs of the period, the Star of Bethlehem is combined with either a single angel or a group of angels. In one wax version, a host of angels with outspread golden wings stand on either side of the stable, with a single star angel hovering above. The tradition that angels should wear a halo was never universal, though many carry a cross and others hold a banner aloft proclaiming 'Gloria in Excelsis Deo'.

A few eighteenth century angels are almost naked but wear a form of draped cloth, reminiscent of their classical antecedents and are tall and slim, while others are fat cherubs with small, budding wings. In the mid-eighteenth century, paper cribs were made, sometimes with fabric laid on the surface of the characters to represent clothes. With their stylised poses, these figures are reminiscent of the characters in toy theatres. Because the quality of crib and presepio angels varies so much, from works of art to cheap items that could have been purchased from market stalls or a pedlar's basket, they form a collecting field with a wide range of prices.

The most ornamented angels are those dating to the 1830s and '40s and made of wax. These are unusually small and have tightly curled white sheepskin or woollen wigs. The clothes are especially attractive, as they were made of brightly coloured scraps of silk and brocade, decorated with gold braids, sequins and glass beads. Some of the South German cribs contained dozens of these figures and they were available singly or in small groups, so that the angelic host could be added to each year.

From the great church presepios come the larger angels, which either flew against clouds, a midnight sky or stood, guardian-like, on pillars to the side of the stable. Flying angels were always barefoot and have their feet in different positions, whereas those intended to stand have the usual holes in the feet so they could be pegged in position. The finest have large, carved wings while others have embossed card or even paper. All are now hard to find as there are so many collectors who specialise in angels, in addition to those who are completing a presepio setting with a heavenly host.

One type of Christmas angel belongs specifically to Germany and is believed to have originated in the period just after the Thirty Years War (1618-48). The story tells how a Nuremberg doll maker named Balthasar Hausser, full of grief because his little daughter, Anna, had died of plague during the war, honoured her memory by making a very special angel.

Far left: A wax Christ Child is arranged in a velvet-covered box, with a grotto-like scene made of gilt foil, silver foil and mica. The box lid is glass, with a frosted greeting 'Buon Natale' and was an expensive form of Christmas greeting. c.1870. 3 ¼in (8.2cm) x 4 ½in (11.4cm).

Left: A typically German representation of a child-like angel, with mica sprinkled wings, postmarked 1905.

Above left: Christmas Children were invariably beautiful and shown in romantic surroundings. The girl with her dog was published by Stewart and Woolf and printed in Prussia. Postmarked 1904.
Courtesy Angela Owen

Above right: St. Nicholas with his attendant helper, who carries a candle-lit tree. Dated 1905.
Courtesy Angela Owen

The child had told her parents that she had dreamed of an angel with curly hair, who wore a crown and a bright red and gold pleated skirt:, with great wings reaching the ground. Her father remembered the description given to him by his dying child and dressed one of his dolls in a foil skirt with golden wings. The story is curiously detailed and has probably been adapted and changed over the years, but it does provide an explanation for the so-called Rauschgoldengels (gold foil angels) which are peculiar to the Nuremberg and Sonneberg areas. In one print of the 1770s, a Rauschgoldengel is shown standing within a wreath and holding a candle in each hand.

Rauschgoldengels, so called because the word rauschen means to rustle, take different forms, as they were adapted to fashionable types of doll, so that early nineteenth century examples have papier mâché heads, while those made

Made of thin sheet brass, the Rauschgoldengel wears a crown. Traditionally, the angels are without arms but are made in a variety of styles. This version has a German shoulder head, c.1900. Ht. 8 ½in (21.6cm),

In many 19th century paintings, the angels are more like pretty children with their wings added as an afterthought. Both palette and drawing become softened. Alexander Maximil Seitz (1811-1888). *Courtesy Christie's Images*

around 1900 are sometimes made of pink bisque. At some periods, the dolls had arms and legs, so the limbs were dispensed with, while at other times the stiff, pleated skirts formed stands that supported the heads. In all probability, the angels developed because the manufacture of thin sheet brass and gold was a speciality of Nuremberg and Fürth, though it is more romantic to believe in the story of the dying child.

Mid-nineteenth century Rauschgoldengels always wore tall, decorative crowns and were often placed in the centre of the Christmas tree, invariably with a belt of crossed ribbons at the waist. Sometimes, a flowered headdress is worn rather than the traditional crown and the angel carries a garland of flowers which forms an arch over her head. Variations are still made today, though most now wear some kind of cape and the whole figure is dressed in paper, rather than the expensive beaten metal of old.

The gold foil angels were particularly suited for use on the Christmas tree, as they were light in weight, making it possible to use large versions. In the last quarter of the nineteenth century, chromo-lithographed, embossed paper faces began to be utilised in place of the conventional doll's heads, which made the angels even lighter, and some are found carrying a printed Christmas tree instead of candles. Gradually, the Rauschgoldengels became so popular that they were made in several parts of the country.

The cherub-like angels, which flew among the branches of trees across Europe and America in the mid-nineteenth century, also originated in Germany, where they were made in composition, wax and papier mâché. The most expensive were well-moulded in papier mâché, with tiny gilded wings and painted hair. Though the waxes are interesting, they are both crudely modelled and decorated and were originally cheap. Occasionally a finer version is discovered, with applied paper decoration or sequinned robes and wings, though those appearing on the market seem to have been produced for the cheapest shops. The most inexpensive tree angels were made after 1880 and were simply cut-outs, rather like paper dolls, but with brightly coloured wings.

Flying, worshipping, blessing or playing musical instruments, all angels were disliked by the Protestants, who recoiled from their obvious Catholicism. To the Baptists, Calvinists and Presbyterians, images of saints, angels, Mary and the Magi had no place in plain worship. While many a parent relented a little and allowed children to decorate a tree, angels were banished. Martin Luther, with his more sympathetic approach, is reputed to have introduced the Christ Child as a gift bearer in Germany and, very slowly, the tree angel began to take the form of a pretty child with wings, rather than a celestial messenger.

The child-like dolls produced by the German toy industry in the second half of the nineteenth century were ideal for this type of figure. With sweet faces and golden mohair wigs, the dolls were costumed in muslin and lace and given a star or crown to wear on the head. Most of those intended for the European market have tinselled wire and gauze wings and are very much in the manner of a child-angel but for British and American families, wary of the taint of 'Popery', the doll was changed into a fairy and given a wand to carry. Gradually fairies became more worldly and have mischievous faces and broad, very un-godly, smiles. The transition from angel to fairy seems to have occurred around 1845, as the only fairy-type figures of British origin that can be dated before this time are those made of paper and probably not intended for Christmas trees.

The rationalism of the eighteenth and early

Above left: A tinted photographic card with a curious interpretation of the Christkind shown in the stable with a lighted Christmas tree

Above right: In German families, the older sister was dressed to represent the Christkind, who brought gifts from the Infant Jesus. Sweetmeats were set out under the tree. Postmarked 1911.

The English toy maker, Chad Valley, turned its attention to the manufacture of tree fairies in the 1930s. She carries the original wand and has gauze wings. Marked with a Chad Valley foot label. Ht. 12in (30.5cm). Courtesy Constance King Antiques

Christmas dolls are often a combination of fairy and child. This German bisque headed girl, c.1895, has an open mouth and composition body. The original costume, with a circular cape, conical, tinsel trimmed hat and woollen gold-decorated coat, reveals her intention as a tree ornament. Ht. 9in (22.9cm).

nineteenth centuries would have discouraged any belief in fairies among educated people, as did the various Protestant churches, but in the second half of the nineteenth century they became the subject of many stories, writings and experiments, so that, by the 1890s, the fairies of Walter Crane and Arthur Rackham were acceptable in sophisticated circles. These later versions were elegant and stylised and led to a much more imaginative and artistic approach to their design, culminating in the sinuous, fantastical images of the 1920s.

When Charles Dickens wrote 'A Christmas Tree' in the magazine *Household Words* in 1850, though he referred to 'that pretty German Toy, a Christmas Tree', he did not endow it with the holy symbolism it was accorded in Germany but described it as pervaded with a 'fairy light' and talks of longing to return to the magical ambience of the tree, 'of wanting to live forever in the bright atmosphere I have quitted; of doting on the little Fairy, with a wand like a celestial Barber's Pole, and pining for a Fairy immortality along with her. Ah, she comes back in many shapes, as my

In this brightly coloured German card, the Christkind stands beside Mary and the Infant Jesus, while winged, disembodied angels hover in the light that pours from heaven.

Right: The Angel of Christmas, represented by a pretty girl. German, c.1912.

eye wanders down the branches of my Christmas Tree, and goes as often, and has never yet stayed by me'.

When British dollmakers created fairy dolls, they made the adaptation from angel to fairy by dressing the figure in frocks rather than draped robes or shifts and shortening the lengths, so the legs below the knee were visible. The haloes disappeared, to be replaced with crowns, stars or tiaras and the long angels' wings became wired gauze additions, with no pretence of any form of realism but completely in the idiom of theatrical or fancy dress. It was probably the influence of theatre that inspired the costumiers to cross silver ribbon on the legs and arms of the dolls and supply a generous sprinkling of sequins and beads that shine in candlelight.

Though we now think of fairy dolls as relatively small figures, some of those found in original costume are surprisingly large and presumably stood at the foot of the tree, while smaller versions were hung from the branches. With an eye to this, German dollmakers soon adapted their standard dolls into fairies for the British and American Christmas markets and marked examples are found from all the leading bisque doll makers. As waxed composition was both cheap to produce and created a very lightweight doll, this material was popular for export, despite the hazards of placing dolls that would melt on a tree that was lit by candles.

Some of the small solid wax tree angels of German origin have spun glass wings, which give them a curious, insect-like quality. Spun glass formed an attractive decoration for papier mâché fairies, which were gilded or painted and are popularly known as 'Dresdens'. These tiny figures were made in the most perfect detail and resemble little precious gold and silver trinkets but were cheap enough to be sold in markets or bazaars.

Angel's Hair, originally made of the most delicate spun glass, gave a romantic, snow-like effect to the

The Fairy Doll had become an essential feature of the British Christmas by 1870 and German manufacturers costumed dolls of all kinds to satisfy this market. This bisque headed SPBH 1909, c.1910, wears the original tinsel decorated costume and carries a wand. Unlike most fairies, her hair is brown. Ht. 12in (30.5cm).

Right: Larger fairy dolls were needed for the tall trees that were popular in the late 19th century. Made in the Sonneberg region of Germany, c.1890, this waxed composition has an open mouth with small teeth and an abundant mohair wig. Her muslin dress and small wings are trimmed with tinsel. Ht. 18in (45.7cm).

Christmas tree. The use of this white, gauze-like decoration developed from an old German folk tale which recounted how, each year, all the animals sat around the Christmas Tree, except for the poor grey spiders, who were constantly swept away by the busy housewives. As a last resort, the grey spiders asked the Christ Child for help. Once he knew of their predicament, he let them into the house, where they crawled everywhere, up and down, around the branches, until the great Christmas tree was covered with spiders' webs. Because the Christ Child knew that housewives hated spiders' webs, he turned all the cobwebs on the tree into gold and sliver, so that the

children could enjoy the visit of the angels once a year.

'Spun' glass, which is in fact a type of glass thread, could be wrapped around the simplest card or paper figures, to provide an aura of light and it is sometimes found in combination with chromolithographed figures of angels, as was tinsel, which so often outlines the fabric wings of fairy dolls and was used to decorate the Christmas tree itself with swags and loops. Tinsel had originated in France in the sixteenth century, when it was used particularly for the decoration of military uniforms. In this early form, very thin copper wire was wrapped around with silver or gold and this was then wound around thicker cord to give the effect

An English poured wax fairy, c.1840, a gilt butterfly on her head, costumed in expensive gold lace, spangles, beads and silk. This doll hung on the family Christmas tree of ancestors of the actress Anna Neagle. Ht.7in (17.8cm).

Christmas children are often a curious amalgamation of angels and idealised, beautifully dressed winged girls. German chromolithographed scraps, c.1885

of a thick gold or silver rope. Much cheaper forms of tinsel-making were developed, particularly in the Nuremberg area and by the mid-nineteenth century, it was made of lead. A variety of different substances, including cellophane, can be woven into tinsel which is, essentially, a twisted thread holding short lengths of reflective material.

In Germany, some of the twentieth century Christmas dolls, though they look fairy-like, have in fact developed from the Christkind, the Christ Child, a curiously indefinable presence, part holy, part a human child with a celestial presence. In the celebration of Christmas in some Catholic areas of Germany, the windows were always left open on

Christmas Eve so his presence could enter the home. Because Martin Luther disapproved of the old traditions of St. Nicholas, the Christ Child, the embodiment of all that was fine and pure, became generally accepted in Northern Germany as the principal gift-bringer for children.

The concept of a beautiful Christkind, wandering the world on Christmas Eve, searching for cold hearts he could melt with his love, was both uplifting and alluring, causing the idea to spread with German families to America, where this title developed into 'Kriss Kringle', a character that has also changed over the years. In Germany, the Christkind is not a representation of the child Jesus but is thought of as

Blue and cream were the most popular colours for angels. This Italian terracotta angel, c.1780, has carved wooden hands and sandalled feet. Ht. 19in (48.3cm).

The Christkind in Germany was often an older sister, who dressed up in wings and a long robe on Christmas Eve. c.1895
Courtesy Angela Owen

In a long white robe, the winged Christkind in a stylised setting offers a pantin to an infant. Published by Raphael Tuck. Chromolithographed in Prussia, c.1905. *Courtesy Angela Owen*

St. Nicholas with his winged Christkind helper, delivering toys and a tree. The wings of the child are much more realistic than usual. Postmarked 1909.

Christ's messenger, usually portrayed by a young, fair haired, angelic girl. In the nineteenth and early twentieth centuries, the visit of the Christkind was still enacted in homes where there were young children and is still repeated today in traditionalist families. The moment when a fair haired girl, dressed up as an angel figure in white, with golden wings, stepped into the house through the open window was always magical. Through the darkness and silence of the night, the Christkind entered the room with a draught of cold air, which seemed to pierce the hearts of adults as well as the believing small children. As all the lights were extinguished, it was not hard for children to believe that the white figure was a spirit sent by the Baby Jesus

himself. In some villages in the 1890s, a figure would walk along the street, stopping at any windows left open, but not entering the room, a tradition that is now only remembered by the act of leaving the windows of the room where the Christmas tree stands open a little, just before midnight. In some parts of Germany, the children left messages on the window-sills on St. Nicholas Eve, so that the saint could take them with him to the Christ Child.

Christkind figures, always with golden curls, sometimes appear on Christmas trees but were more usually found on Christmas cards or in the form of lithographed scraps. The concept of the Christkind was virtually unknown in Britain, so that any figures of this kind used to be thought of as fairies or angels but have in fact a much more elusive and fascinating genealogy. Sometimes the holy messenger left a few scraps of silver paper or a few sequins on the stairs, if the room where the tree was set up was difficult to approach through a window. Other families rang a special bell, used for no other purpose, at the Christ Child's approach, yet another association of bells and Christmas-tide.

Some of the traditions of the Christkind are replicated in the Swedish celebration of St. Lucia. This saint's day, on 13th December, sets all the Christmas celebrations in motion. Late in the afternoon, just after dark, a child would dress up in a long white robe with a traditional red sash. The St. Lucia figures are always immediately recognisable from the Christkind by the presence of this sash and. above all, a curious headdress of seven lighted candles, intertwined with evergreens. Wearing her St. Lucia crown and accompanied by other children wearing white robes and paper hats, this Christmas spirit does a good deed in serving the adults with coffee and biscuits. Some of the crowns were especially made and very fine – in this century, American versions were occasionally lit by electricity, though this must have spoiled the excitement of wearing the hazardous crown of candles.

Angel, Christkind, Fairy doll and St. Lucia had become oddly confused in the imaginations of the public and many artists by the 1890s, resulting in some curious amalgamations of form, though all represent the essential innocence and wonder that cannot be absent if Christmas Eve is to cast its two thousand year old spell on Christendom today.

By the late 19th century, angels in the image of women could guard, warn or chastise. The ornate wings became part of the costume design of the elongated figures. John Melhuish Strudwick (1849-1937).

Courtesy Christie's Images

CHAPTER V
Dressing The Christmas Tree

'Look at the tree, the rough tree dazzled
In oriole plumes of flame'
C. Day Lewis

Carrying a silvered chromo-decorated gift box c. 1905 and a paper
snow child of the same date, the German bisque headed doll stands
before a synthetic silver and white tree, made in 1969.

On 27th December in 1845, a very special Christmas treat was held by the London Mission Society at the Temperance Hall in Cripplegate, London – over four hundred children were invited to the 'Exhibition of the German Christmas Tree, or Tree of Love'. A reporter for *The Illustrated London News* commented that this was the usual mode of celebrating the Birth of Christ in Germany. 'In almost every family is set up this pleasing figure, having the resemblance of a growing tree, loaded with a profusion of fruits and flowers: and upon its branches the different members of the family suspend the little presents which they intend for those they love best: and on the exhibition of the tree the presents are claimed by their donors and handed, with compliments, to their friends.'

English people in 1845 were still attempting to work out the rituals of the Christmas tree, which was generally considered to be one of young Prince Albert's not entirely welcome additions to life. Albert had sent to Germany in 1840 for a very large tree and it was decorated to delight his wife and their baby girl and to remind him of the Present Room he had enjoyed as a child. The London Mission Society had hung oranges and other fruit, as well as hundreds of presents on their tree, the whole being illuminated with a myriad candles. Obviously there was no thought of decorating the tree with baubles or strings of beads and the old German tradition of a Tree of Paradise with fruit and confectionery was followed.

There are few references to Christmas Trees in the advertising pages of newspapers and magazines before 1840 but from this time there is much more emphasis on gifts for children. 'Do, Papa, Buy me Punch's Locomotive Picture Gallery. 240 changes for 2/6' or 'What Fun. Follits Funny Roundabouts and Laughing Stock'. Because of Prince Albert's influence, the way in which British people celebrated Christmas changed completely from a period of adult conviviality, with much feasting and drinking, to a German-style children's festival. An 1846 writer noted that the tree was the most important feature of Christmas Eve in Germany, though there were some differences in observance between the Protestant and Catholic provinces. 'It is almost a matter of surprise that so pretty a custom has not obtained a more general footing in England, especially as the lighting up of the Christmas tree was regularly practised in the family circle of the old court, when the children of George III were young.'

In Germany, wax tapers, bonbons, cakes, gilded nuts, apples and ribbons were hung on the tree, to make it as gay and brilliant as possible, the decoration varying in splendour with the wealth of the family. The writer also comments that the custom of dressing a girl as the Christkind, with a gilt crown and wings, was beginning to die out, 'many thinking it irreverent, besides involving a deceit into which the elder children are obliged to be admitted as partners'. Despite the dire warnings about the end of Christmas, it was at this time that the decorations industry was established, particularly in Germany, where the manufacture of tree ornaments became associated with the already established toy industry. By 1848, when the Royal children's Christmas tree at Windsor Castle was described in British and American magazines, an assortment of specially made containers and decorations was already being made. Elegant trays, baskets, bonbonnières and other receptacles for sweetmeats of all forms, colours and degrees of beauty were utilised on the royal tree, as well as the more usual gilt gingerbread and eggs filled with sweets, and

Attractively coloured lithographed tinplate clips, decorated with scenes of children playing. German, c.1880. Ht. 2 ½in (6.3cm).

'Young's Xmas Tree Tapers', with red and yellow candles in the original box, c.1910. Trees have been lit with candles since the earliest times.

hung from the branches with coloured ribbons. On the top of the tree stood an angel with outstretched wings holding a wreath in each hand. The trees at the castle were arranged on Christmas Eve and left in place until Twelfth Night. During the period, two similar trees were set up on the sideboard of the Royal Dining Room and lit by many candles. Price Albert chose the decorations for Queen Victoria's tree, while the Queen spent much time in re-creating for him an exact copy of the Present Room he remembered from his childhood at Rosenau.

By 1854, writers in magazines were commenting that the erection of Christmas trees had become a general fashion in England, and that they were available in large quantities in Covent Garden market in London. In many schools and family parties, the tree became the centrepiece. At St. James District Schools in Hampstead Road in London, the tree was lit by twenty two gas jets and decorated with toys and little silk bags, containing sugar plums. After the Christmas party, the children all received a toy and a bag of sweets and the next evening twenty-six poor old women were given flannel petticoats and packets of tea and sugar as gifts.

Supporting the British position in the Crimea, Christmas trees began to be decorated with flags, a curious patriotic addition that died out after the First World War. Because trees were such a novelty in Britain, they were described in detail, especially the German custom of a large tree surrounded by several smaller versions. The central tree was often hung with brilliant ornaments and knick-knacks, Chinese lamps and flags and banners of all nations, the Turkish supported by the French and British. There was a fashion in the mid-nineteenth century for standing the trees on a sheet of mirror, increasing the effect of the circles of small trees that varied in form and decoration.

Between some trees were baskets filled with fruit and moss, as well as vases of flowers. At the four corners were huge Yule logs, covered with holly and ivy. Much less attractive to the modern taste were the groups of game that were prepared for one tree by the taxidermist from the Natural History Department of the Crystal Palace.

A set of paradise fruit, made of painted, delicate glass, including grapes and raspberries, and still contained in the original thin cardboard box, c.1900.

Coloured cotton batting was used to represent the costume of this tree figure of a snowballer with a bisque head, c.1900. Ht. 2in (5.1cm). Courtesy Angela Owen

One massive central tree of the 1850s was lit by gas lights with fruit-shaped shades. The fruit and flowers on the tree were made of opal glass, which was found to be ideal for lighting purposes. The grapes, lilies and flowers were patented by F. Bartlett. Just a few years later, in 1857, Rimmels in the Strand were suggesting flower and birds' nest decorations which were perfumed for the Christmas tree, while gelatine lamps in various colours for the tree could be purchased from Field on Wigmore Street. 'Ready filled' Christmas trees that were 'warranted to last for years' were sold on Charlotte Street in the West End of London for 7/6d each.

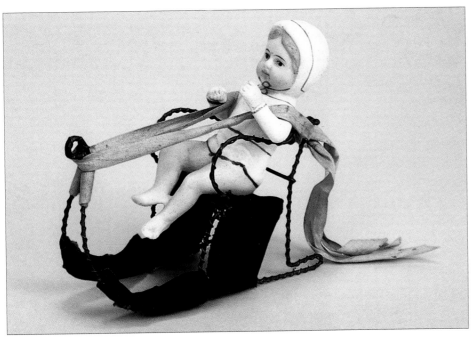

An all bisque boy, riding in a wire and velvet sleigh and with the original ribbon type hanger. Made in Germany, c.1890. Ht. 3 ½in (8.9cm).

Right: Carrying a bunch of holly, this yellow cotton batting child has a bisque head, c.1885. A variety of similar figures in different colours were often packed in boxed sets. Ht. 2 ½in (6.3cm).

Most of the mass-produced decorative devices that became common after 1860 have their inspiration in the shapes of fruits, biscuits and flowers that had been used on Christmas trees since the late eighteenth century. One tree, set up in Nuremberg in 1795, was so large that the branches spread wide under the ceiling so that people could stand beneath and look up at the angels, dolls, animals and fruits, which were all made of sugar. Soon papier mâché, wax, wood, china and glass were used to manufacture re-usable tree ornaments, which were exported from Germany in vast numbers, particularly to America, the wealthiest and fastest growing market.

Porcelain figures form the rarest group of decorations, as their weight and fragility led to rapid breakages. Bisque and glazed porcelain cherubs and angels with moulded hangers are the most frequently found, though there is also an assortment of snow children, Father Christmas figures and many animals and birds. To classify as a tree decoration, the china figure must have a moulded loop of some kind or as part of the design have a section to which a hanger can be attached. Most of the china tree decorations are unmarked, other than with a number or the 'Made in Germany' stamp used after 1890. Some are of extremely fine quality, with delicate colours and detailed painting, but after 1900 the type of decoration became simpler and the items were obviously made for the cheapest outlets.

There is an equally wide variation in the quality of papier mâché ornaments, with the later pieces, particularly those made in the first half of the twentieth century and representing comic or cartoon characters, being supplied to the poorest sector of the novelty trade. From the 1870s to 1910, one exquisite range of detailed ornaments appeared, known

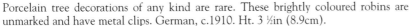

Porcelain tree decorations of any kind are rare. These brightly coloured robins are unmarked and have metal clips. German, c.1910. Ht. 3 ½in (8.9cm).

Right: Larger cotton batting figures resemble dolls as much as decorations. The celluloid mask face girl with a muff is mica-decorated for added sparkle. German, c.1910. Ht. 6 ½in (16.5cm).

popularly as 'Dresdens', from the part of Germany in which they originated. These highly collectable figures, which resemble large silver charms because of their detail and variety, were made of embossed card, moulded under extremely high pressure, decorated with gold or silver paper and finished by painting, lacquering or decorating with sequins or beads. Made in the Dresden area and Berlin, these animals, angels, birds, musical instruments or even vehicles, were made in the round or as virtual silhouettes. A few in a debased form, finished with aluminium foil, were made in the 1950s and '60s but these bear very little relationship to the exquisite trinkets which were finished in now dark gold and silver and decorated with silk threads, angels' hair, tiny satin flowers, ribbons or tinsel. The American market absorbed most

of the output of good quality decorations and Dresdens are now hard to find in Europe, especially as they have formed their own collecting field for so long.

The main centre for the manufacture of these attractive trinkets was Neuruppin, though they are invariably termed 'Dresdens' from the general area, a term that is used in Germany as well as America. The shapes were pressed in the factories and then finished and decorated by outworkers. Though most are single figures, there are rare two and three part Dresdens, such as a pair of horses which pull a sleigh, a group that was further embellished with feathers and fur. The skilled homeworkers who created these charming items so cheaply were not available after the First World War, as the Germans gradually became more unionised and expected better pay and conditions, so

Dresdens are much rarer in Europe than America. Pugs of all kinds are especially popular. This pressed card hanger carries a stick and gloves. German, c.1895. Ht. 2 ½in (6.4cm).

the manufacture died out. It is their basic ingenuity that holds so much appeal: the cotton wool, silk cords, coloured feathers, tinsel and scraps of fabric all combining into alluring models.

Some of the simpler designs used for Dresdens were later utilised when celluloid became fashionable, though this material, being so inflammable, was soon discarded, so that early models are now collected eagerly. Despite the obvious danger, celluloid was used for lanterns and fairy dolls, as well as fishes and birds with hangers on their backs. The late Japanese versions can be identified by their bright colours and less detailed modelling and were exported to America in particular during and after the 1914-18 War, when German products were no longer available. Fine celluloid pieces were made in America between 1930 and 1940, especially by the Irwin Co. of New York and Chicago; though celluloid toys were made in Britain, there seems to have been little interest in the manufacture of decorations that depended on a skilled, but low paid, work force.

Early prints of decorated German Christmas trees reveal many large figures which could have been made either of paper or wax. Flat wax tablets in red, brown or cream were made in several areas of Germany, but particularly in the South. Wooden models for these figures can be seen in several museums and collections and have complex detail, such as the pattern of fabric or embroidery that gave a rich, textured surface. Similar, but much simpler, versions were made for gingerbread, which was sometimes decorated with gilded or coloured paper. On some trees, cut paper animals and figures were used, as well as the so-called host wafers, the Oblaten. Christmas biscuits and cakes made in decorative form especially for hanging on trees were traditionally finished with simple paper woodcuts, or prints in one or two colours, but with the introduction of chromolithography in the 1850s, a new world opened, especially as the chromos could be embossed and cut in a single process by the 1870s.

The flowers, birds, snow scenes and Santa Claus were fixed to the various types of biscuit with a sugar

Bisque butterflies clipped to the tree are reminiscent of the decoration of trees of Paradise. Unmarked. Made in Germany, c.1905. Ht. 4in (10.2cm).

Below: With a circle of green glass and sections of cut rod hung with silvered beads, this tree decoration was made in the Lauscha region, c.1885. Ht. 6 ½in (16.5cm).

Above: Lauscha tree hangers, made of delicate beads, are jewel-like in effect. Because of their fragility, they are now rare. German, c.1885. Ht. 6in (15.2cm).

Left: Glass and ceramic beads were sometimes combined to make decorative tree hangers. German, c.1910. Ht. 3 ½in (8.9cm).

After the complex glass shapes were blown or moulded, silver nitrate was swilled around inside to create the effect. This swan with a feather tail is also decorated with painted detail. German, c.1910. Ht. 4in (10.2cm).

solution and were inevitably removed and saved by children so they could be glued into scrapbooks. The decorative tree biscuits were never as popular in Britain as in America and Germany, where some very large examples, over twenty inches high, were produced. The designs originally used on biscuit papers were gradually adapted by the printers of scraps, though the traditional subjects of the Christ Child, angels, knights and medieval ladies soon gave way to baskets of puppies, prettily dressed children, ships and nesting birds. A few chromos were printed in pairs so that, glued together, they formed a hanging tree decoration, embellished with tinsel or mica to give added sparkle. The single-sided tree versions were obviously extremely fragile and relatively few have survived from the millions which were produced, so the majority of collectors now concentrate on the chromos themselves, which are often in pristine condition, as they were preserved in scrapbooks.

Folded honeycomb tissue balls, fans and bells made before the 1914-18 War are equally hard to find, as they were especially fragile. Early versions were sewn rather than stapled and have deeper, much richer colours, sometimes with several shades on the individual sections of colour. Small round fans, curious figures, stars, bells and balls were produced in small tree sizes, though these are even harder to find than those made to hang from the ceiling.

Glass was the ideal material for replicating the real fruits and sugar ornaments of the old German Trees of Paradise, as it was relatively light and could be textured in imitation of frosting, satin, oil, silver and gold. Spun glass tails and wings, fabric leaves and silk flowers gave added interest to the plain blown glass forms. Some of the earliest tree decorations were made from sections of glass rod, which was wired to form glass cradles, bird cages and spinning wheels. Usually made of white glass in combination with blue or green, the hangings, though made in several areas, are commonly termed Lauscha ornaments. Of all tree decorations, those made of glass are the most effective and the most fragile. To find a complete angel or an icicle whose tip is unchipped is always a surprise. The first recorded mention of a British Christmas tree decorated with glass ornaments relates to that erected at the Crystal Palace in 1854, and designed by Mr. Hurwitz. The arrangement was assembled in three layers, the tree itself standing on a platform and loaded with a variety of brilliant ornaments and knick-knacks and a profusion of large and small Chinese lanterns. This tree stood on a large mirror-covered platform, which reflected the ornaments and gave the scene sparkle and brilliance. The whole tree was gas lit, the bright light further thrown from the fruit which decorated the tree. The fruit and flowers were made of opal glass, which was found to be best adapted to the purpose, and bunches of grapes, roses and lilies were all designed by F. Bartlett, who was in charge of the Natural History Department at the Crystal Palace.

Perhaps the fame of this splendid tree, spread through

prints and reports in the newspapers, encouraged more families to arrange a tree of their own, though references to any domestic use of glass ornaments are hard to find before 1860, and it seems that, in general, trees were decorated with the traditional gilded nuts, confectionery, foil and net-covered gifts.

An 1848 German glass order book refers to 'Six dozen Christmas balls in three sizes', but it seems that the new style decorations took a while to become established and more extensive advertising is only found in the 1860s. 'Oh, Papa! Do send to the German Toy Company for our Christmas Tree ornaments. The largest and most varied assortment in the world in 1/-, 10/- and 20/- cases.' Herr Specht, the manager of the shop at Walworth Road in London sent the orders with great speed by land or sea. The number of such advertisements increases rapidly after 1865, reflecting the growth of trade with America and Britain. Early baubles are in very short supply but can be recognised by the weight of the glass and the heavy, ornate brassed hangers.

In nineteenth century Germany, there was a rapid expansion of the glass industry following the Napoleonic Wars, the main emphasis being on coloured wares. The Thuringian region, rich in raw materials for the glasshouses, had become important in the eighteenth century, its development being encouraged by the Electors of Saxony, and the more prestigious work commissioned by the court at Gotha. The region of Lauscha became linked to the production of inexpensive glass, its first glasshouse having been established in 1597 mainly to produce containers for apothecaries.

The blowing of Christmas tree ornaments is believed to have developed from the manufacture of glass beads. Bead making began in Lauscha after 1755, though the original industry had begun in Nuremberg in the sixteenth century. In Lauscha, the folk workers obtained small quantities of glass from the big glasshouses and blew the beads in their own homes, using the bagpipe method, where the bellows is held under the arm. Their products were used mainly in the fashion industry and 'pearls', made by filling blown glass beads with wax, were popular. The blown glass beads were originally the chief product of Lauscha and were among the first decorations made to festoon the Christmas tree.

From the end of the eighteenth century, small decorative figures, such as animals and birdcages, were also made and grouped under the term 'toys'. Boar hunts, gardens and markets were made in glass, though it is

Spirit lacquered metal tree clips, with concealed candle holders, remain one of the most secure methods of fixing candles to tree branches. Probably German, c.1885.

difficult to know whether these were intended to be hung from trees. Several of the early designs, such as that of a stag hunt, continued in production into the twentieth century and at the Erfürt Museum there are miniature dishes, chandeliers, babies in cradles and many birds. It was a simple matter to adapt such pieces to tree decorations by fusing on a loop of glass, though in some instances, the figures were fixed at the base to a metal holder, so that the toy could be clipped to a branch.

Glass icicles are believed to have been made from the mid-nineteenth century and are among the most lovely tree decorations, their twisted and knopped shapes being made in an infinite variety and enclosing delicate spirals of colour. Icicles were made by twisting a rod of glass and fusing on a hanging loop. The manufacture of the most complex ceased in the 1930s, though clear glass versions are still made.

Coloured glass baubles have survived in much greater numbers, the earliest being clearly recognisable because of a cork used to fill the neck. Some very large versions were sold throughout the year and are popularly known as 'witch balls'. As the technique improved, the cork was substituted by an embossed tin cap, which was gilded or brass finished. Some of the

Cupids and angels in white bisque were produced in vast numbers by the German porcelain factories. Some were sold in boxed sets, each figure in a different position, c.1890. Ht. 4 ½in (11.4cm).

Early tree baubles are characterised by their heavy metal hangers. c.1900.

early balls were lead coated on the inside, which gave a lovely dark silver finish, while in others the lead was allowed to run unevenly over the inner surface and behind this, where the glass remained clear, a layer of brightly coloured wax was poured, giving a variegated effect. These early baubles were heavy and were fixed to the trees with wire. As methods of blowing thinner-walled shapes developed, it became possible to produce large assorted boxes of hangings, such as those offered by Kilian Müller Ph. und Sohn of Lauscha, who advertised 'Glass Christmas Decorations. The most beautiful ornaments for the Christmas Tree. A varied assortment consisting of 300 pieces of splendid glass fruit, birds, bells, fruits baskets, air balloons, angels with glass wings and lace, some balls richly covered with chenille, novelties, fantasy forms, candle holders and icicles. All for the very low price of five marks.' Müller offered a free gift of a Christmas Crib, with twenty-four plaster figures and the Gloria, with each order.

The building of a gasworks in Lauscha in 1867 made it possible for the glass-blowers to work with a very hot and well regulated flame and from this period the ornaments became thinner and more even in substance, losing the attractive imperfections of the mid-nineteenth century work. These new, lighter baubles were cheaper, as they used less glass and the makers became more adventurous both in colouring and modelling. 'Punched in' versions were made by re-heating the blown ornament and pushing in a wooden shape or a piece of coal, while the blower sucked out air at the same time. These early punched versions can be recognised by their irregularities of shape, the later versions being made in a plaster mould. As the industry developed, it was forced to become more organised, with merchants such as G. Söhlke of Berlin, who advertised himself as 'a Royal Court Supplier' gathering together products from homeworkers and producing a catalogue that was carried by his agents across the world.

The German agents in the main cities of Europe and America were extremely important for all spheres of the Christmas decoration industry, as they listened to buyers' comments and sent back to Germany any new ideas or developments in fashion that could be incorporated into their selection for the next year. They also observed the ranges of competitors and set up displays at trade fairs. At the agents' showrooms, sample boxes and displays were always available and there was keen competition to attract the buyers for Schwartz of New York or Gamage's of London. This constant battle for even lower priced decorations was eventually to stifle the individuality of the workers,

who were forced to simplify designs for the mass market. The trade buyers placed their orders a full year before and the homeworkers began creating American orders in December, for shipping in May.

The Thuringian makers did not have any real competition in the nineteenth century, as no other European country could match their low prices and Sonneberg trade reports from the 1870s and '80s tell of a fast expanding business. In the years 1888-89, the Sonneberg Chamber of Trade and Industry commented that Christmas Tree decorations had taken over the primary position held previously by the

Cotton batting, crêpe paper-covered girl in a bathing dress and carrying a sponge. The face is chromolithographed. This type of piece was time-consuming to make, which adds to its appeal. American, c.1900. Ht. 5in (12.7cm).

Good quality china tree decorations are still made by Wedgwood in their famous jasper, combining an old tradition with a modern design.
Courtesy Wedgwood.

Below: Musical instruments remain a popular subject for decorations. This silvered glass bugle was made in the Lauscha region, c.1900. Ht. 6in (15.2cm).

was thrown on to another wheel, where it was spun to a fine thread. Trade catalogues referred to this substance as 'magical hair' and it was used to give birds and angels an ethereal effect. Though the figures embellished with angels' hair look so atavistic in style, many were made in the 1920s, so the clips are often one of the best methods of dating.

The rounded sections of baubles, birds and nuts were made in two-part moulds that allowed for bold ornamentation, which could be highlighted with bright colours. Early decorations were silvered by the use of lead or made entirely of coloured glass. Other effects were achieved by a sprinkling of mica, held in position with gelatine. The old method, of using lead mirror for backing, was abandoned in the last quarter of the century and silver effects were achieved by the use of silver nitrate mirror. The liquid silver was poured into the plain glass balls, swirled around and then poured out, to be used in the next decoration. The work was the province of women, who also added the decorative devices, such as tinsel, scraps, feathers and chenille.

Sometimes several glass shapes were combined with

production of glass toys in general, though obviously, for many merchants, the two products were complementary and both appeared in their catalogues.

In a museum exhibit at Erfürt, a showcase type sample can be seen, which was assembled from local work by Carl Bohm Caspar of Ernstthal and Rennsteig. He offered 'Constant novelties in glass Christmas Tree ornaments plated with genuine silver…Easter, Advent and Christmas bells as well as other hanging decorations.'

Some of the more ornate pieces are fine examples of folk art, with the designs derived from other local crafts, such as straw-work and metal comb-making. There are splendid glass birds with long spun glass tails and angels with large, glass-fibre wings. The glass threads were spun off the hand-turned wheels the workers kept in their own cottages. The glass rod was held to the flame and stirred with another glass rod. With a swift movement of the hand, the molten glass

Glass tree ornaments, including birds with spun glass tails, strings of beads, a silvered ball and painted fruit. Made in Germany, c.1905.

coloured threads or dusted with gold and silver, to give a snow-like effect. Fruit was often painted in oil colours and fabric leaves were added. From the two part plaster moulds, hundreds of figures were turned out, Father Christmas in red, green or silver robes, witches, Chinamen, the Man in the Moon, a Madonna and Child, flowers, leaves, balloons, airships and eventually motor cars. The most expensive blown ornaments were always the top pieces, made to crown the tree: these were often complex and could combine angels, candle holders and turned, wrought iron-like effects, reminiscent of local ironwork.

A traveller in 1902 commented that, when he looked down into Lauscha from the railway terminus at night, every house was lit by long blue points of flame, as the people laboured over their gas burners. The men blew the glass, using a simple tread-bellows under the work table, while the women coloured and painted the decorations. Even the smallest children were set to work, cutting off the long necks after blowing and fixing on the metal clips. The German Christmas decoration industry was founded on this low paid, but highly concentrated, family labour and it inevitably declined rapidly in the twentieth century, because Japanese imports flooded the American and European markets and the workers themselves were demanding better conditions and higher wages. Thuringia was always the poorest region of Germany, with more than its fair share of genetic defects, tuberculosis and rickets, the diseases of deprivation. Against the dark, and often tragically short, lives of the makers of Fancy Goods, the shining, ephemeral tree decorations form another tonal contrast in the sometimes disquieting tapestry of Christmas.

CHAPTER VI
The Festive Board

'Power laid his rod aside
And ceremony doff'd his pride'
Sir Walter Scott

Children's Christmas plates remain a popular gift, especially those illustrating Beatrix Potter's engaging Peter Rabbit.
Courtesy Wedgwood

In Victorian times, though Christmas foods inspired many writers and illustrators, the stark reality of the servants who toiled, the animals which were killed and the garret workers who created beautiful packaging for madam to throw on the fire after a single glance, cannot be forgotten. Today, it is easy to disregard the dark side of Christmas, hidden behind brand-name packaging, trussed poultry and rarely seen farm animals: vast herds, whose lives are lived in concrete and steel. Before 1850, the centres of all the big cities were busy with droves of oxen going to market, the sounds and smells of the slaughter houses and tanners, the sweetness of sugar, boiling in the back rooms of candy stores. Butchers hung their poultry, row upon row, in the open air outside their shops, while the carcases of animals were decorated with ribbons, wreaths and, invariably, sprigs and bunches of holly. In London, the grocers, with their delicious dried and preserved fruits, nuts and marzipan cakes, hung flags from their windows with pictures of John Bull and his family eating their Christmas dinner with the slogan 'There's a good time coming' – but not for everyone,

Goose and duck remained the traditional Christmas meat for most British people until the mid-19th century. Many artists began to paint winter scenes for calendars, magazines and music covers. George Dunlop Leslie RA (1835-1921), c.1865.

Courtesy Christie's Images

though during the Christmas season many vagrants and beggars did well by moving into the cities, as begging was easier when rich businessmen were full of seasonal good spirit.

Before 1840, the celebration of Christmas was relatively low-key, with various local traditions and some singing and feasting. In country districts, the wassail bowl, puddings and cakes were produced for the feast but, in general, ordinary people were not rich enough to lay in vast stores of expensive French and

The food and games of an English family Christmas in the 1840s. There are holly, plum pudding, ribs of beef and a decorated and iced cake, but as yet no tree. Published by Dean and Co. Threadneedle Street, c.1840.

Below: Christmas hampers were advertised throughout the 19th century and enabled families in reduced circumstances to accept food as a gift without any loss of dignity. By G.G. Kilburne and published in the *Illustrated London News* in 1873.

Italian preserved fruits, while cooking several courses of a hot meal over a kitchen fire in a cottage was a near impossibility. The extension of the railways, improvements in roads, the installation of kitchen ranges in smaller houses and the gradual increase of the middle classes, with more money to spend on their families, all encouraged people to enjoy the holiday. Christmas itself attracted increased public interest in the early nineteenth century, when its old traditions and associations began to attract antiquarians, such as William Hone, who in *Ancient Mysteries Described*, published in 1823, cast his eye on carol singing, which was unknown in Scotland since the time of John Knox, but was still practised in Wales, where carols were sung to the accompaniment of the harp.

Attractively bound books of carols became popular as gifts, because drawing-room music played such an important part in Victorian social life. In 1822, Davies Gilbert's *Collection of English Carols* had appeared, followed in 1833 by William Sandys' *Christmas Carols*

Large display pieces are popular, especially when toy and decoration are combined. The carton, felt covered reindeer has metal antlers and the sleigh is wood, with a carton and fabric Father Christmas and ornamental crackers. c.1890. Ht. 9in (22.9cm).

Ancient and Modern. The traditional carols, such as 'I saw three ships' and 'The first Nowell' were of some antiquity, though the world's great favourite, 'Silent Night', was not composed until 1818 and was based on a traditional Austrian tune. Between 1850 and 1880, a large quantity of Christmas music contributed to the atmosphere of benevolence and good cheer, which became an essential part of a Victorian celebration that was suffused with family love and church worship. Despite nineteenth century romanticism, fostered in particular by the writings of Charles Dickens and Sir Walter Scott, this new type of celebration could not have flowered without the ancient pagan traditions that underlay so many rituals, particularly those relating to feasting.

The medieval Christmas was characterised by strict fasting during Advent and riotous feasting on Christmas Day, when vast quantities of roast meat and liquor were consumed. Henry III's Christmas dinner in 1247 included boar, partridges in pastry, peacock, hare, swan, fowls, oysters, rabbits, mullet and conger eel. The fashion for stuffing one bird with another began in this period, when it was customary for the centrepiece of the feast to

be carried aloft with great ceremony among the guests. An attempt to preserve the beauty of a live peacock was made by skinning the bird before cooking and then, after stuffing, usually with smaller birds, the washed skin was laid over, with the claws, beak and crest: sometimes the whole bird was then gilded. Though peacock was only occasionally served in the Victorian period, the old ceremony is recorded in the medieval style prints and paintings, which were so popular in the 1890s. The Carrying-in of the Boar's Head is another favourite subject, the representations suggesting that the tradition had survived from medieval times, though in fact the boar had become extinct in Britain by the late seventeenth century and it was usually replaced by a pig's head, with an apple or orange in the open mouth. Queen's College, Oxford, continues this ancient tradition by carrying in the head on a massive silver dish, presented to the college in 1668 by Sir Joseph Williamson. The ceremonial includes trumpeters and a choir which sings the 'Boar's Head Carol'. After the chief chorister is presented with the orange by the Provost, sprigs of rosemary are handed around.

The killing of pigs and boars for Christmas was

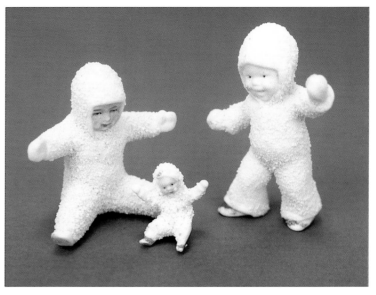

It is rare to find such a complex cracker still complete. The dog has a composition head and the rabbit is of cotton batting, c.1900. 10in (25.4cm) long.

Snow Babies were especially popular in America, where they were used for scenes as well as on cakes. c.1905. Ht. 2 ½in (6.3cm).   Courtesy Angela Owen

China Father Christmas jugs were often part of an advertising promotion and must have brightened many Christmas tables. This piece is marked 'W. England', c.1935. Ht. 4 ½in (11.4cm).

A large Snow Baby, with an unusually detailed face and wearing painted brown shoes under his hooded suit. c.1910. Ht. 3 ½in (8.9cm).   Courtesy Angela Owen

Snow Babies with touches of colour on the costumes are popular. This example has painted features. c.1912. Ht. 2 ½in (6.3cm).   Courtesy Angela Owen

common throughout Europe and was a practical as well as a celebratory ritual. In most cottage families, the pig was killed in late November, as fodder was difficult to obtain during the very cold months. It was for this reason that so many other beasts were slaughtered in the Anglo-Saxon Blot-Monath – the slaughter or sacrifice month. Sacrifices and slaughter were inevitably accompanied by drunkenness and feasting, so that though the origins of the Saturnalian celebrations were overlaid with Christian compassion by the mid-nineteenth century, country people still perceived the slaughter of a pig as an excuse for celebration. For the Christmas feast in middle-class homes, a joint of ham could be dressed with marchpane (marzipan), chocolate and macaroon, a curious recipe that was suggested in a cook's dictionary of 1830.

With the reintroduction of wild boar farming from Germany to Britain, it is likely that the ancient tradition of eating this meat at Christmas will re-emerge. This beast is particularly associated with the season of feasting as the god of peace and plenty rode on a boar and the heroes of Valhalla feasted on the flesh of the animal after it had been sacrificed to Freyr. There are several versions of the Boar's Head Carol and

A small jug, possibly part of a set, with polychrome transfer decoration. On the back 'A Handsome Hostess, Merry Host / A Pot of Ale and now a Toast'. Green Royal Doulton mark, c.1930. Ht. 2in (5.1cm).
Courtesy Angela Owen

Though the quality of German white bisque figures had declined, the subject matter became more interesting, when contemporary motor cars were incorporated. German made, c.1930, but for the English market. Ht. 3 ½in (8.9cm).
Courtesy Angela Owen

the ceremony is replicated in other colleges and institutions where idiosyncratic rituals are observed. The story surrounding the ceremony at Queen's College seems to rely more on schoolboy humour than historical accuracy, but provided an excuse for an excellent piece of pageantry. A student of Queen's was attacked by a wild boar on Christmas Day long, long ago. Like every good scholar, he was reading Aristotle as he walked along and he used this volume to choke the beast. Forlorn at losing the book, he cut off the boar's head to retrieve it and then carried the severed head in triumph to the college High Table.

Boar's heads, peacocks and hearty joints of beef appear on Christmas cards, gift-box lids and seasonal prints, as do the various types of wassail bowl. Writing in 1823, Hugh Hughes records that in Wales on Twelfth Night, there was an ancient custom of 'making a wassail, namely cakes and apples baked and set in rows on top of one another, with sugar in between, in a type of beautiful bowl which had been made for the purpose and had twelve handles. Then warm beer, mixed with spices from India, was put in the wassail'. The liquid at the top of the mixture was drunk in turn by the men sitting around the fire. When the ale was finished, the pudding-like wassail was shared.

Wassail bowls originating in Herefordshire and Gloucestershire are usually of the twelve-handled form, while the Welsh Folk Museum, at St. Fagans, has several varied examples. Some, in addition to the looped handles, are decorated with birds, berries, oak leaves and other figures, all made of roughly-potted local clay. The Ewenny Pottery was still producing wassail bowls in the twentieth century in traditional designs for special occasions. Wassail seems to have been concocted, like

Pre-Reformation mince pies were a savoury mixture of meats and spices and characterised by a pastry figure of the Christ Child laid on the crust.   Courtesy Jane Vandell Associates

punch, from the best ingredients that were available. In the Shetland Islands, egg yolks, beaten with sugar, cream and brandy, made 'whip coll', while in parts of England cider, heated and mixed with spices and eggs, was used. The most popular mixture, known as 'lambswool', was made by mixing ale, roasted apples, sugar, spices, thick cream and bread. Some wassails were gargantuan, like that at Jesus College, Oxford, where ten gallons were consumed from a silver-gilt bowl. The wassail was carried around the houses in country districts, accompanied by a group of revellers, sometimes in fancy dress or with blackened faces, who sang carols and invited everyone to drink from the bowl in exchange for money, food or even more alcohol. A number of small lignum vitae bowls have survived and it was this type that was most likely to have been carried around with the singers. In parts of Wales, wassail bowls were made of ash, a wood that is always associated with the birth of Christ.

Because punch was easier to make than any form of wassail, it became accepted in a variety of guises across Europe and America. In 1599, the Colonel-in-Chief of the Navy used eighty casks of brandy to make a punch which was served from a vast marble bowl and whose fumes were so strong that the boys serving the liquor had to be substituted every fifteen minutes. The red-cheeked Father Christmas, holding aloft a wassail or punch bowl on a Christmas card, is himself a descendant of an equally early tradition, the appointment of a Lord of Misrule, who supervised all the music, revelry and feasting.

Some of the seasonal foods were eaten over the complete holiday period and were originally substantial dishes. Our modern mince tarts, over-sweetened and encased in soft pastry, are an insipid copy of the robust pies which were, in the fourteenth century, filled with game, mushrooms, spices, offal, beef and broth. Originally, the pie seems to have been a stand-by which could be eaten at any time during the twelve days of Christmas, and until the Reformation it was baked in an oblong shape. Because the top invariably sank in

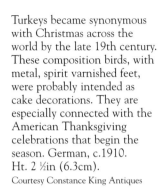

Turkeys became synonymous with Christmas across the world by the late 19th century. These composition birds, with metal, spirit varnished feet, were probably intended as cake decorations. They are especially connected with the American Thanksgiving celebrations that begin the season. German, c.1910. Ht. 2 ½in (6.3cm).
Courtesy Constance King Antiques

cooking, a pastry figure of the Christ Child was laid on the top, which added to its seasonal popularity. Despite its somewhat coffin-like form, the mince pie was a substantial meal but fell into disfavour after it was banned as 'Popish' by Oliver Cromwell. By the second half of the nineteenth century, mince pies had made the transition from a savoury to a sweet dish and Victorian recipes suggest mixtures of suet, sugar, currants, port and spices as a filling for tarts that were eaten at teatime or as a dessert.

Though now considered an essential bird for the Christmas feast, turkey did not feature on the European table until the sixteenth century, when it took its place alongside goose and swan. In America, turkeys ran wild in flocks, with some birds weighing up to sixty pounds. Because turkeys are relatively easy to fatten, their rearing was not difficult and there were specialist farms in Suffolk by 1800. Despite their availability, it took a long time for turkey to replace goose on the British table, though in parts of America it was a centrepiece and was served with ham, jams, pickles and mashed, scalloped and candied potatoes as part of Christmas dinner. Before 1900 every part of America celebrated Christmas with its own local meals: antelope and

buffalo steaks in Wyoming and possum in the South. Because turkey became the centre of the family feast by 1900, special plates, decorated with a print of the bird or a festive border were sold for the richer, middle class homes, where it was possible to afford the luxury of seasonal crockery. The turkey was also popular as a subject with the makers of decorations, as its curious shape and brilliant plumage inspired craftsmen to create colourful gift-boxes, cake decorations and miniatures.

As the amount of food and wine consumed at Christmas decreased in response to the more Puritanical attitude of the Protestant church, interest in decorating the home and table grew. Pride in family, the house and its furnishings was especially evident in North America, a fast growing, fairly affluent market which was a magnet to manufacturers of decorative pieces for the table. In the well-ordered households of the late nineteenth and early twentieth centuries, where mother was always in charge of the home and family, meals were an essential part of social intercourse, vast quantities of plate, serving dishes, place-card holders, table centrepieces, and, in America, toothpick holders, were needed every day.

Above: An unusual white bisque snowman wearing a conical hat, c.1910. Ht. 3in (7.6cm).   *Courtesy Angela Owen*

Above right: Cake decoration of a winter sports girl in colourful costume. Made in Germany c.1920 and incised '9470'. Ht. 3in (7.6cm).   *Courtesy Angela Owen*

For the Christmas market, which relied on an affluent population with money to spend on frivolities, pressed glass plates and jugs, children's dishes decorated with Santa prints, Father Christmas mugs, cruets and jugs in many qualities flooded the market and now offer rich pickings for collectors of Christmas. In general, those decorated with images of Santa are most popular. Small figures of Christmas elves and children in snow-suits are a close second and were originally used not only on trees and in Christmas villages but also on cakes and puddings.

Gleaming with snow-white icing and laden with pine trees, churches, carol singers and skaters, the Christmas cake itself became a veritable model village. Almost every family could afford some kind of celebration cake, though the British recipe, a rich, damp concoction of fruit, spices and sugar, would have won any world competition for sheer weight. Women's magazines provided inspiration for the more nervous

cooks and encouraged them to create skating scenes surrounded by trees, an animal party, Dickensian coaching days or, in the 1930s, Disney revels with Mickey Mouse. Bisque, porcelain and composition figures were sold not just by department stores and firms such as Woolworth's but by every corner stationer and confectioner, so that a high number have survived, often to be re-used each year and passed down in families. Once plaster and, later, plastics replaced china, the ornaments had a much shorter life, as they became discoloured and the inventiveness of the manufacturers also declined. Many people now collect cake decorations, as they are attractively small and made in such variety that fresh models can always be discovered. The most popular are those that carry some kind of mark, or a maker's number, which helps in attribution, though most are valued on quality and rarity, any larger items being especially collectable.

Among the best known German makers of cake decorations are Galuba & Hoffmann, Limbach, Gebrüder Heubach and Carl Schneider. Santa riding a

Ornaments of this type were used on the table at Christmas and sometimes formed part of a set. This white bisque piece, c.1900, is incised 'Germany 3142'. 6in (5.2cm) long.

Polar bear and skiing elephant, both made in Germany and included in Snow Baby collections. c.1920. Ht. 2 ½in (6.3cm).   *Courtesy Angela Owen*

White winter sports Snow Babies with skis, toboggan and an ice axe. Additions such as these add to their value for collectors. c.1920. Ht. 1 ¾in (4.4cm).
                    Courtesy Angela Owen

bicycle, carrying a Teddy bear or climbing a chimney would be among the more desirable pieces, as the simple standing figures, whose effect depended on colour and quality, are not rare, as they were owned by thousands of families. When skiing became fashionable for women in the early twentieth century along with other winter sports, smartly dressed bisque ladies in bobble caps and children in snow-suits kept the cooks' confections up to date. The fur effect, made by applying grog to the bisque before firing, was used for children and babies, who wore all-in-one snow-suits with hoods and play on sledges and skis.

Snow babies first appeared on the market around 1905 but gained tremendous popularity because of their association with Robert Peary, who discovered the North Pole in 1909. A few snow babies carry a flag saying 'To the North Pole' and there is a strong American tradition that they were made in honour of Marie Peary, who was born on one of her father's explorations of Greenland in 1893. The child was named Marie Ahnighito, but was usually called 'Snow

Baby' in Eskimo. Another version says that she was named Ahnighito after the Eskimo woman who sewed her small fur suit. Though the Peary family later denied these appealing stories, the figures were certainly associated with his journeys. Some of the more complex nodding versions having eight or more tilting heads clustered in and around an igloo. Hertwig & Co. and Galuba & Hoffmann were the most important producers of the babies, which were still manufactured in the 1930s.

Snow babies were made in such a variety of qualities and so many sizes that, especially in America, they now form their own specialist collecting field. Some of the rarest are popularly known as 'Blue Snows' and have blue

Large snow figures are very collectable and this German example in the form of a gnome is also very well modelled. c.1925. Ht. 3 ¼in (8.3cm).
Courtesy Angela Owen

Santa wearing big seven league boots. Glazed porcelain. Made in Germany, c.1910. Ht. 2 ½in (6.3cm).   *Courtesy Angela Owen*

The motorbike makes this bisque Santa especially interesting. Made in Germany, c.1925. Ht. 2 ½in (6.3cm). *Courtesy Constance King Antiques*

tinted grog, others are dolls with bisque shoulder heads and fabric bodies. There are 'Pink Snows', 'Slenders', with slimmer bodies and coloured hair which shows at the front of the hood, jointed babies and tiny versions lying on sledges or rolling on their backs. Any versions over four inches high are very collectable and were intended as table, rather than cake, decorations. The rarest wear polar bear costumes, with the mask of the bear pushed back on the head: some carry animals, bears or Christmas trees. There are associated groups, such as carol singing scenes or bands, and they also appear as candle holders, forming yet another busy area for the collectors of Christmas past.

The snow-like grog finish was obviously felt to be ideal for anything connected with the winter and was used by the German porcelain factories for many ornamental pieces, including angels, spill-holders and Santa Claus' 'fur' suits. Small jardinières were made in Germany especially for the American market and were decorated with grog-covered snow babies and snow scenes of all

Far left: A gilded porcelain sleigh, with a transfer print of Mumbles, a popular seaside village, was both a souvenir and a decoration for the Christmas table. c.1870. Ht. 3in (7.6cm).

Left: Because the icing on British Christmas cakes was so hard, it was possible to use painted decorations of card and composition. The cat scratching a tree is German, c.1910. Ht. 2 ½in (6.3cm).

Snapdragon was one of the most popular Christmas games. Raisins or other fruit were floated in a bowl of brandy, which was set alight. The game was to snatch the fruit without burning your fingers. From an unmarked set of German chromos, c.1895.

kinds. Polar bears were especially appealing when given rough coats and some large sizes were made to stand under Christmas trees or to decorate tables and sideboards. Families who owned these figures exercised great ingenuity in their use, making our modern decoration of the Christmas table seem mean and unimaginative in comparison. Ringing bells, flashing lights and music were all recommended as part of the Christmas tableau for the sideboard in the years before the First World War, though few have survived, as they were often constructed of papier maché and cardboard. Fortunately, more substantial buildings and figures were made for shop windows and were a speciality of the Christmas cracker makers, who supplied retailers with horse-drawn carriages, sleighs and gondolas, all packed with brightly coloured cosaques with loud snaps. Thomas Smith and Co. the most famous maker declared his intention, 'To raise the degenerate cosaque from its low state of gaudiness and vulgarity to one of elegance

and good taste.' He went on to add in his advertisement that his mottoes, instead of the usual doggerel, 'are graceful and epigrammatic'. The gifts concealed in the tissue crackers were usually cheap jewels, toys, tiny fans,

Witches have an ancient association with the Winter Solstice and the celebration of Christmas. The lid of 'Tom Smith's Cracker Box No. 542', c.1895. A label inside reads 'Wright and Son, Refreshment Contractors, Colchester'. Ht. 9in (22.9cm) x 7 ½in (19cm).

'Pudding Charms', with a bell for the old maid and a button for the bachelor. The 'Merrythought', or wishbone is a particularly British tradition, with the symbol of good luck used on many greetings cards. c.1925. Ht. 3in (7.6cm).

Left: Boxed sets of unused crackers are not easy to find. These miniatures contained small white metal charms, as well as mottoes. Made by Brock's of Sutton, Surrey. Set No. 236, Miniature crackers. Box 9in (22.9cm) by 4in (10.2cm). With a 1910 Cadbury's Picture Box No. 740.

perfumes or Japanese curiosities, though the makers could be commissioned to use expensive pieces. 'Millionaire's Crackers' were packed in a solid silver casket and each contained a good piece of jewellery in gold and silver settings. Tom Smith was also responsible for 'A Golden Sheaf' cracker, containing a gold ring set with pearls, the single piece costing £400 in 1905. The most delightfully vulgar were the 'Costly Crackers', each with a ring box in the centre containing gold rings.

The expensive boxed crackers made by Tom Smith and his imitators were descendants of the noisy detonating balls that so infuriated the police in city streets in the mid-nineteenth century. The term cracker is derived from 'Cosques', an allusion to the Cossacks, who fired irregularly, as they had to reload their rifles while galloping along. The transition from street ammunition for the games of naughty children to tasteful ornaments for the dining table was made in 1847

A more affluent middle class was able to afford table centres that were especially made for Christmas. The silvered metal 'winter twigs' could be used for small candles or flowers and evergreens. Each section can be separated and arranged in different ways. Smaller twigs could be purchased separately, so the centre could be extended for tables of any size. English, c.1880. Ht. 18in (45.7cm).

with the establishment of Tom Smith. The first types of table crackers were termed 'bonbons', because they originated in France and had no snaps but were simply sweets, usually sugared almonds, wrapped in coloured paper. Tom Smith seems to have developed the cracker from the two elements and it was soon imitated by German and some French makers, so that unless contained in the original box, they are very hard to attribute to an individual maker. All the manufacturers used boxes edged with lace paper, decorated the tissue with chromos and used similar miniatures as fillers. Box-lids were often designed by well known artists, though some amateur work was used by Smith, who paid three to six guineas for the designs around the turn of the last century.

A visitor to Tom Smith's factory in 1904 described the storeroom as a large curiosity shop and commented on the immense trade that had opened with Japan for the supply of all the curious items that crackers contained. Most cracker-making was the province of women workers. The skilled operative first spread on the work-bench a bright gelatine lining, then the white lining and the ornamental fringed border of the cosaque. The detonator was then laid in the centre and the whole wound around a hollow cylinder before it was passed to the decorators, who packed sets in special themes, such as garden flowers or knights. Complete table settings could be assembled

Both the Arts and Crafts and the Pre-Raphaelite movements fostered clothes and furnishings in the medieval styles that were ideally suited to Christmas. The expensively dressed chidren sing a carol outside the drawing room door. Lady Laura Alma Tadema (1852-1909).
Courtesy Christie's Images

Opposite: A very rare punch bowl made for Christmas between 1875 and 1880 by George Jones and impressed with his monogram and crescent mark: painted pattern no. 3468. The deep blue majolica bowl has a turquoise interior and is moulded in relief with a band of holly. 9in (22.9cm) diameter.
Courtesy Sotheby's Sussex

Wedgwood produce special Christmas plates for the collectors' market each year, with contrasting decoration. These were for 1982 and 1983.
Courtesy Wedgwood

Royal Copenhagen Christmas pieces for 1990, including a tree decoration.
Courtesy Royal Copenhagen Porcelain

around the theme of these boxed crackers, which were decorated with a degree of flair and precision that was only possible when labour costs were low.

In 1913, Gamage's were selling monster crackers, fifty-four inches long, though Tom Smith was happy to create giant models, over forty feet high, for large children's parties. Some of the Gamage's boxes had lids designed by Lawson Wood, with other lower priced crackers based on themes of the Pied Piper, jesters or mermaids. The flower crackers, obviously designed for ladies, were very ornate, with the large flowers made of silk, feathers and beads. As relatively few crackers survived Christmas, any that are boxed are at a considerable premium, as are those which retain the original gifts. The most expensive are pieces such as a car filled with crackers and driven by a chauffeur, or a garden swing filled with angel-decorated cosques. These complex sets are now frequently described as 'window' or 'trade pieces' but they appear in old catalogues simply described as 'table decorations'. Because the centrepiece crackers are both eye-catching and well made and sometimes incorporate good quality toys or models, they are among the most desirable of all the Christmas collectables, made especially appealing because they were the most extravagant – labour-intensive pieces, frivolities, made to be destroyed in a second during the fun and games of the Christmas feast eaten in the shadow of the Lord of Misrule.

CHAPTER VII

Images of a Saint

'Up to the house top the coursers they flew
With a sleigh full of toys – and St. Nicholas too'
Clement Clarke Moore

An American style crêpe paper Santa, in a smart snowsuit and carrying a well engineered sack. Printed in England, these figures were sold on the roll to form a colourful frieze. c.1940. Ht. 14in (35.6cm).

Santa Claus, a saint trailing bacchanalian revelry and a suggestion of misrule behind him, a kindly old man, who can change in an instant into a vicious chastiser of children, a bringer of gifts and punisher of evil, he combines the darkness and light of Christmas in a character that has adapted itself to the changing world. Our first image of Father Christmas is retained throughout life, so parents who do not conjure up his magic in those early impressionable years lose for their children a lingering anticipation and excitement, which lasts through all our days, to be sparked unexpectedly by sleigh bells, red, fur-trimmed robes or the words 'T'was the night before Christmas'.

This old, old man, who possibly never existed, is thought to have been born 280 years after Christ, and became St. Nicholas of Patara, Bishop of Myra and the patron saint of Russia and Greece. His early years are clouded by legend, but he is imagined as tall and thin, with a stately, noble manner, despite his shyness of character. Because of the gentler aspects of his nature, he was venerated as a protector of anyone who was in trouble or distress. Saint of a diverse group of merchants, sailors, thieves, judges and children, St. Nicholas was born into a wealthy family and of a Christian mother, though she died when he was young. Because he refused to worship the statues of the Emperors of Rome, he was imprisoned in 303 but released when Constantine became Emperor. Nicholas was philanthropic with wealth, and disguised himself so he could help those in financial distress. He became Bishop of Myra when he was still very young, an event that, in itself, was something of a miracle, as the bishops in council could not decide on who should be appointed and finally recommended that anyone who

Santa has little connection with the aesthetic hooded saint. German chromos from a scrapbook, c.1895.

St. Nicholas only occasionally appears in a purple robe, which adds to his interest for collectors. German chromos, c.1900. Ht. 4in (10.2cm).

came into the cathedral whose name was Nicholas should be chosen. Perhaps because of his youth, the bishop became popular and was said to have performed such miracles as raising a sailor from the dead. The most famous story, and one that associated him with pawnbrokers, concerned three young noblewomen, whose father had lost all the family money, so they were forced to remain unmarried because of their lack of a dowry. Nicholas crept to their windows three times

The many faces of Santa Claus, wearing costumes of different colours. From a 1900 scrapbook.

at the dead of night and left a bag of gold for each of the sisters in turn. In some versions of the story, he placed the money in a stocking, while in others it was rolled in a ball and sometimes he is said to have thrown the gold down the chimney. The saint was very critical of the recipients of his bounty, so that anyone of an evil or lazy disposition was not helped, an element of his character that combined well with nineteenth century morality, which hinged on the rewarding of virtue, either in this world or, all too often, in the afterlife.

St. Nicholas is typical of the many mysteries and contradictions of the Christmas season, as there is no solid evidence that he lived at all, or that any of the

Father Christmas becomes much more human in his behaviour by the end of the 19th century and is portrayed less as a saint than as a genial grandfather, who carries presents.

A superb shop display Santa in colouful lithography. When key-wound, Santa's head, eyes and hand rock from side to side, as does the toy horse in the foreground. Made in Germany c.1890, such rare items are centrepieces for any Christmas collection. Ht. 23in (58.4cm).
Courtesy Bonhams

events in his life took place as recounted or that he ruled with a morality more in line with medieval beliefs than those of the fourth century. What is fascinating about the saint is the gradual evolution of his character and the way we still accept him as a perfect man, despite the passing of nearly two thousand years and our acceptance of him as legend rather than fact. His calm beauty, his unassuming attitude, his use of great wealth to help his people, his willingness to assist the fallen, irrespective of their crimes or shortcomings, his concern for the welfare of children, all combine to create an ideal of humanity that is as pertinent today, despite our materialism and cynicism, as it has remained in each succeeding century. That is the essential and enduring miracle of St. Nicholas.

When Bishop of Myra, St. Nicholas rode a fine white horse and was revered because of his patrician, yet kind and gentle, manner. The embroidered bishop's robes were doubly impressive on Nicholas because of his height, which was accentuated by the mitre and

and bringer of gifts. His tomb soon became a centre of pilgrimage and, in 1087, a group of merchants and sailors from Bari in Italy sailed to Myra to retrieve the saint's remains. Each year, a festival is held in Bari to commemorate the return of Nicholas, the saint who possibly never was.

Because he was the patron saint of children, Nicholas' popularity became so great in the medieval period that the church authorities became worried that he had become more important in children's lives than the Infant Jesus. Martin Luther, in the sixteenth century, was particularly concerned that St. Nicholas should not be venerated after the worship of saints had disappeared in the Protestant Reformation. Luther's German Protestantism was much gentler than that of

Despite the Christmas tree roped to his back, Father Christmas manages to test the girl's reading ability, though he has already delivered his gifts. German chromo, c.1900.

because of his youth, which contributed to the beauty of his appearance. Legends seem to have sprung up around this saintly man from his earliest years, such as the story of the innkeeper who murdered three boys, dismembered them and hid their remains in a vat of vinegar. Nicholas discovered the deed and, by prayer, re-united the bodies and restored the children to life. The fame of this saintly Bishop spread across Europe, together with the stories and legends associated with his life and his very human qualities: his love for the poor, gentleness, rewarder of good, rescuer of children

This version of St. Nicholas is very collectable, because of the quality of the composition head and the unusually realistic 'fur' that trims his robe. German, c.1885. Ht. 9in (22.9cm).   Courtesy Angela Owen

Benign St. Nicholas, who has found two ordinary children in the snow and regales them with gifts. Postmarked 1911.

'Heureux Nöel' from a very human St. Nicholas. Fancy dress costumes for Santa were popular from the 1890s and appeared in many mail order catalogues. French. Postmarked 1912.

Wearing an unusual green robe, Santa has a holly wreathed hood and holds a young fawn, a reference to the animal that leapt away to tell the shepherds of the birth of Jesus. c.1912.
Courtesy Angela Owen

his counterparts in Britain and Switzerland and he showed a more sympathetic understanding of ancient traditions and beliefs, so instead of sweeping away every aspect of the old Catholic Christmas, complete with St. Nicholas, he encouraged children to believe that Christmas gifts were brought instead by the Christ Child himself. The Christkind soon developed from an abstract concept into the figure of a beautiful, angelic girl, believed, in Protestant homes, to be the messenger of the newly born Jesus. Like one of the stories of St. Nicholas, she enters the room through a window on Christmas Eve and leaves her Saviour's gifts for good children. Because the morality of not rewarding bad children, thought to have been practised by St. Nicholas, appealed so much to the Protestant ethic, this element of Christmas was perpetuated in North Germany by the introduction of a strange and

frightening character, Pelze-Nicol, Fur-Coated Nicholas, who accompanied the Christkind when she visited families on Christmas Eve to remind her of all the shortcomings and sins of the little ones. If the children were exceptionally bad, Pelze-Nicol would leave the parents a switch or rod for their chastisement.

The traditions of the Christkind and Pelze-Nicol were taken to America with the many waves of German immigrants, especially to Pennsylvania, though over the years the girl's name was gradually changed from Christkind to Christkindle and so to Kriss Kringle. Pelze-Nicol is an especially curious character, who seems to have developed out of man's inherent need to have some tangible figure to represent evil. The Protestant Reformation, in its more excessive manifestations, conjured up almost as many horror figures with the heart of the devil as had existed in the

Far left: Santa at the North Pole and on top of the world. Designed in England and printed in Germany. Published by Misch and Co. Dated 1913.
Courtesy Angela Owen

Left: Santa surrounded by eager, happy children is the archetypical Christmas image. He lifts his finger in admonition as the game becomes noisy. German, unmarked, c.1880. Ht. 12in (30.5cm).
Courtesy Angela Owen

Below: Somewhat gnome-like, this lively Santa in a white tunic and matching trousers tips his gifts to the floor with his blue-gloved hands. Ht. 12in (30.5cm), c.1900.
Courtesy Angela Owen

medieval church, though they were often more abstract in form. Gradually, Pelze-Nicol developed a much uglier character in Knecht Rupprecht, or Ru-Kas, Rough Nicholas. This figure always carries a cane to punish bad children and in Germany he questioned them with great severity about their general behaviour and their knowledge of the catechism. By the mid-nineteenth century, Knecht Rupprecht always carried a bag and trailed a noisy chain, so the children would tremble as they heard his approach on Christmas Eve, knowing he could read their innermost thoughts. Wearing a suit of animal skin and sometimes carrying a bell as well as his rod and sack, the figure must have terrified little children, especially when a hideous mask was worn. In the early days of the twentieth century, his huge eyes were sometimes lit up by electricity and flashed when Knecht Rupprecht was especially angry with a recalcitrant infant.

Knecht Rupprecht seems to have much closer associations with ancient diabolism, or the dualism that beset the early church, than kindly St. Nicholas and also has a strange dual genealogy. He is associated in some way with the god Odin, the Gift bringer, who also punished evil and rewarded good and was said to have ridden an eight footed horse of magical powers, which galloped the midnight sky. Odin and his horse Sleipnir were obviously connected in the minds of country people with Pelze-Nicol and there are many variations on

Right: Wearing a gold robe, Santa carries a goose feather tree. For ease of modelling, his arms are often folded. Papier mâché. Made in Germany, c.1885. Ht. 8 ½in (21.6cm).

Below left: Wearing a Russian-style hat, this Father Christmas dressed in a red robe carries two sacks of toys. German chromolithograph, c.1900. Ht. 10in (25.4cm).

Below right: Rupprecht type animal masks were intended to frighten young children. Some later versions had flashing electric eyes. A few bisque headed dolls have heads of this type that drop over the girl's face. German, from the Sonneberg area, c.1890. Ht. 9in (22.9cm).

this character. In some German towns and villages, Knecht Rupprecht alone brought the presents on Christmas Eve and wore a white robe, a flowing beard, a mask and high boots. The open window, letting in a sudden blast of cold air and the sound of bells and chains in the street, alarmed children, even before the masked figure entered, with the message that his master, Jesus Christ had sent him. He not only listened to their catechism but questioned the parents as to their conduct through the year. Fortunately, most children gained his approval and, after their initial fear, they were presented with the gifts from the Christ Child in Heaven. For the very few bad children, a rod was handed to the parents, with Pelze-Nicol's instruction that it should be used frequently. Obviously the fancy dress and stagecraft could only have worked on the youngest children and, by the 1880s, the whole performance was reserved for the under sevens, with the older children acting parts with their parents. This strange, fur-clad devil figure who serves the Christ Child has other names, such as Hans-Muff or Krampus. He had no representation in Britain, partly because there was little present-giving before the nineteenth century, Christmas being celebrated as an adult, rather than a children's, festival.

In Britain, the feast of St. Nicholas, on 6th December, was characterised by feasting and

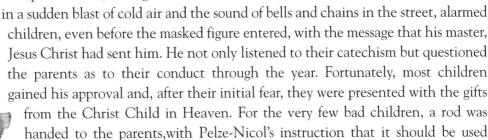

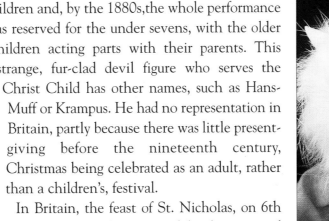

With an embossed card face and covered in a red crêpe paper robe, this Father Christmas carries a tree. German, c.1900. Ht. 5in (12.7cm).

nineteenth century illustrations, the character 'Christmas' carries a bowl of punch or wassail, is crowned with a wreath of holly and wears fur or fur-trimmed robes. The British 'Old Christmas' has obvious links with the ancient Lord of Misrule or Master of Merry Disports, who was chosen to create merry havoc in the homes of noblemen, in the Oxford and Cambridge colleges and the Inns of Court, until swept away by the Puritans.

The Lord of Misrule was frequently represented as a kind of Punch figure, wearing a parti-coloured suit and a pointed hat, often decorated with bells. At other times, he is a jolly, bearded and robed master of ceremonies, who either wears a crown or a wreath of evergreen, usually holly. Charles I in 1635 knighted the Lord of Misrule who had been appointed by the Inns of Court, largely because he spent £2,000 out of his own pocket to make his tenure of office memorable. Normally, the Lord of Misrule organised games, entertainments and masques at the noble houses, where his mandate was to prevent anyone sitting apart 'in pride or self-sufficiency'. Shakespeare's 'Fool' was completely in this idiom, playing on the concept of a man who is clever enough to make a clown of himself. The Lord of Misrule was sometimes chosen by chance, one of the favourite methods being to bake a cake containing a gold ring: whoever received the slice with the ring being appointed master of ceremonies, a tradition which was perpetuated in the good luck charms and the silver sixpences hidden in the family Christmas puddings.

Pagan revelry and Christian celebrations were still combined in the eighteenth century British Christmas, though there was gradually an increase in the amount of present-giving. Largely this was practical in nature, with masters giving clothing to servants and children receiving books or a few toys. In poorer households, the season was mainly celebrated by special meals and drinking. Fortunately for children, the festival was

celebrations, with roots in the pagan rites of the Saturnalia. In 1616, Ben Jonson refers in his 'Masque of Christmas' to a character known as 'Old Christmas' and 'Captain Christmas', who was announced by the beating of a drum. Old Christmas wore a high-crowned hat, doublet and hose, cross-tied garters and carried a truncheon. The characters of 'Old Christmas' and 'Weihnachtsmann', the Christmas man, in Germany have associations with both St. Nicholas and Odin. In

changing gradually, along with attitudes to education and the management of the nursery. There were more printed games and illustrated books, more push- and pull-along horses, more doll's houses and toy kitchens. These toys were available to children from ordinary homes, as well as the very rich and there was a corresponding softening of parents' attitudes to their young: no longer were they mere possessions, to be used as pawns in the marriage stakes or troublesome creatures, to be swept out of sight as often as possible, but were important in their own right and deserved special treatment, with their own nurseries, simple clothes and, ultimately, their own festival, presided over by Father Christmas.

German children had enjoyed their festival long before it was adopted in British and American homes. The British Christmas was heavily influenced by German traditions, brought to England by the Hanoverian monarchy and to America by the thousands of German immigrants. In 1821, the first American book about Christmas was published and showed St. Nicholas sitting in a sleigh pulled by reindeer. *A New Year's Present to the little Ones from Five to Twelve* is interesting, as it reveals how many of the Christmas traditions were already established – stockings hanging up for presents, the sleigh being pulled by reindeer and St. Nicholas himself. Washington Irving in *Knickerbocker's History of New York*, published in 1809, describes St. Nicholas as the patron saint of the Dutch, riding in a wagon over the roofs of houses and pausing to drop presents down the chimneys of children once a year. Irving gave his 'Christmas' a Dutch type low-brimmed hat, tights and a pipe. Despite the portrayal of a typical New Yorker of Dutch origin, the character is also described as a 'jolly elf, skyward bound, with a pack on his back'. Irving in America, like Sir Walter Scott or Charles Dickens in Britain, gave interest to the whole concept of an 'old style Christmas' that, in reality, had existed for very few

Ringing his hand bell, this pressed, embossed carton Santa with an easel back wears an American style snow suit scattered with mica and carries a tree. c.1925. Ht. 20in (50.8cm).

people. Fortunately for the memory of St. Nicholas, there was a curious change of mood in the early nineteenth century, led by the investigations of antiquarians, who began to compile books of legends and folk lore and by travellers, who brought back and published accounts of the German and French celebrations of Christmas and the New Year, which gave romance to the season and encouraged the middle classes to develop their own family rituals and ceremonies.

St. Nicholas and 'Old Christmas' would have remained separate characters to the present, were it not for Clement Clarke Moore (1779-1863), professor of Greek at a New York Theological Seminary. Moore enjoyed writing poems for his six children and, in 1822,

Chenille became popular for tree figures from the early 1920s. These elves have celluloid faces and clamber around a Märklin doll's house chimney piece. Santa elves were popular in America and Scandinavia. Ht. 2½in (6.3cm).

The small sleigh, packed full of toys, could be heard sliding across the roof and then as father spun away from the window, St. Nicholas slid down the chimney and bounded into the room. Dressed in fur and carrying a sack of toys on his back, he resembled a pedlar but had merry, twinkling eyes, cheeks like roses, a beard as white as snow and a pipe clenched between his teeth. He winked conspiratorially at father but said nothing, though his round little belly shook like a jelly when he laughed.

It seems that Moore, being a theologian, was diffident about his poem, but a copy was sent to the Troy Sentinel and it was published in 1823. Within a few years, the poem, with its description of Santa Claus, was known in families across America, who welcomed this Christmas character, which appealed to people from all cultural backgrounds. After the

possibly slightly influenced by *A New Year's Present*, he spun a delightful tale beginning 'T'was the night before Christmas'. The poem, known by heart by generations of children, goes on to describe the mouse-quiet silence of Christmas Eve, the children's stockings hanging by the chimney and the peace of mother and father, relaxing by the fire. Suddenly, they are startled by a clatter on the lawn. Rushing to the window, they see a sleigh and eight reindeer in the moonlight. Driving the sleigh is 'St. Nick', who called his team, Dasher, Dancer, Prancer, Vixen, Comet, Cupid, Donner and Blitzen. St. Nick exhorts the reindeer to dash away, 'to the top of the porch, to the top of the wall'.

Father Christmas has a cold journey through snow to deliver gifts to children across the world. German, cotton batting with a composition face, c.1895.

122

A large clockwork nodding Santa, c.1895, made in Germany for display in a shop window. He has a pressed papier mâché head and snow covered boots. The mechanism runs for several hours without re-winding. Ht. 20in (50.8cm).

country where people from many cultures had to be given a sense of identity. In this respect, Santa Claus can be seen as one of the primary figures that helped to cement a distinct American nationality.

Santa's image became firmly established when Thomas Nast, the political cartoonist, began a series of drawings of him for *Harpers Weekly Magazine*. Nast believed that the figure he drew represented St. Nicholas, rather than Santa Claus, but he costumed him in a fur suit and hat, decorated with a sprig of holly and gave him a long pipe. Unlike the tall, aesthetic saint, his figure is usually as small as the little children to whom he talks and he can fly and communicate with nursery rhyme characters. Nast's first Santa was drawn in the 1860s and, during the Civil War, he showed Father Christmas delivering presents to the Union troops. These drawings exaggerated his jolly appearance, by making him very fat and dressing him in a fur suit. At various times, in cartoons published over a twenty-two year period, Santa carried a variety of items, from a record book to a telescope, but he always remained a very happy, benign character. He began to wear a bright red suit trimmed with fur in a coloured cartoon drawn for McLoughlin Bros. and it is this type of suit, with many variations, that is now usually recognised as typical of the American Santa. When the famous toy store, Schwarz, drew Santa for their 1876 exhibition of Christmas toys, they dressed him in a fur suit with a conical hat, a wide belt and carrying a toy-filled sack, while in front of him was a sledge pulled by reindeer.

In Europe the secular American Santa Claus, in his snow-suit type outfit, and the more saintly Father Christmas, dressed in a long, monk-like robe, have existed side by side or been amalgamated in various ways. The concept of a sleigh pulled by reindeer was obviously appealing to children, so this was adopted for Father Christmas, as was the genial nature of the American character. By the 1860s, Father Christmas figures were on sale in Britain, though the only

introduction of Santa Claus, Christmas gradually became more secular in character, presided over by this genial figure, from whom all taint of Popery had been removed. Perhaps this American-style Santa was too sanitised, too far removed from his Christian origins, but his appearance on the stage was opportune in a

123

St. Nicholas' costume evolved from the hooded robes worn by monks. Red, trimmed with ermine, became most popular in Britain and America. Printed on card, Father Christmas has a selection of googlie-eyed dolls, c.1925.

Right: Ho! Ho! Ho!' cries the American-style Santa as he rings his bell. These pressed card figures, sprinkled with mica, had easel backs, so they could be free-standing or hung. They were produced in a variety of sizes. Probably British, c.1920. Ht. 19in (48.3cm).

references seem to connect them with confectioners, rather than toy shops, and we have to assume that they were made of sugar or marzipan. Henry Schwarz is said to have been the first shop in America to employ a live Santa Claus, for their Christmas toy display in the early 1860s, a fashion that soon spread across the world and was especially favoured by the newly fashionable big department stores that were opening in the great cities.

The first toy figures and dolls were produced in the same period, with Harpers Bazaar in 1869 offering a range of models. Their large Santa Claus was dressed in crimson robes and wore a flowing white beard: 'he bears a small Christmas tree made of iron pipes that are to be lighted with gas'. Other, smaller Santas, dressed in grey garments covered with snow were especially made 'to stand beside a Christmas pine' and cost

between $8 and $12. Godey's Ladies' Book, as early as 1868 was beginning to offer instructions for doll-type tree ornaments with papier mâché heads and arms, representing 'Old Father Christmas', though with a body made from five pine cones, this character seems to hark back to a more Saturnalian tradition.

The period 1870-1914 offers the Christmas collector some of the richest pickings, with figures of Santa in any materials being market leaders both with regard to popularity and value. Papier mâché toys of all kinds were a Sonneberg speciality and from this part of Germany Father Christmas figures in all sizes marched across the world. The earliest were made in simple, two part moulds and show Father Christmas standing on a rocky or moss-covered base and wearing a long, hooded robe. Fur or fur fabric was sometimes used to decorate the robe's edge, though more often these areas were painted to represent fur. There was no tradition of a red robe in Germany, so white, green, yellow, purple, blue and crimson are all found, the rarest being coloured black or pink. Mica was sprinkled over the figures to give a snow-like effect and the face is always that of an elderly man with white hair and beard. They carry a goose feather tree, a piece of bog heather or a sprig of greenery. Most are from six to eight inches tall but some, very rare, examples can be over twenty inches, though made in an identical manner in two-part moulds. Early figures have better painting of the features, though the size and rarity of the robe colour affects current value more than antiquity. Sometimes the robed section lifts right off the heavy boots, so that sweets or gifts could be concealed within.

By the 1880s, Santa Claus and Father Christmas figures, though still made mainly in Germany, had evolved into much more complex structures, which were activated by clockwork. One small walking Santa carried a bag of toys, another drove a reindeer with a nodding head, while another played a tune. Almost every kind of toy was adapted for the Christmas market, so the child could choose between a Santa Jack-in-the-box, a Kelly or Santa in a sleigh. Some of the larger nodding clockwork figures have roughly

Pulled by a team of reindeer, a green-robed Father Christmas delivers toys and a Christmas tree. German. c.1910.

St. Nicholas developed into a benign, grandfather-like figure, who not only loved children but showered them with gifts. c.1890.

production was geared to the American market, with the buyers for the big stores demanding an ever cheaper but attractive product. Lauscha had a large and successful cotton wadding industry, which supplied the makers of fruit, flowers and figures for the Christmas trees with base materials for their craft. The cotton wool batting was moulded, rolled, wrapped around card cores and glued in layers to represent snowballs, animals, children and, above all, Father Christmas. Though the colour was normally applied when the model was complete, in some instances self-coloured cotton wool was used. Hundreds of different decorative devices made the figures interesting: some have papier mâché heads, others are gift boxes, others carry trees and have a layer of mica to make them sparkle in the light.

A few batting figures were made in Britain and America after 1910, though the designs were not as ingenious as those originating in Frankfurt or Lauscha, where tinsel, ribbons, flowers, beads and tissue paper all added to the richness of effect. Boxed sets of batting figures were made up of numerous characters, including Father Christmas, a group of angels or a set of helper elves. Such groups are now extremely scarce and most collectors are happy to buy individual pieces, which were made in such variety.

With the introduction of motor cars and, later, aeroplanes, Santa took another leap forward and was also found suspended from an air balloon or driving an engine. There were limits to what the most ingenious creators of batting figures could do and they were gradually replaced by the tin, celluloid and cast iron toys, produced for play as well as display. One of the rarest of all Santa toys represents a sleigh pulled by goats, which cantered up and down as the toy was moved along. Cast iron mechanical Santa banks are now highly collectable, J. & E Stevens in America producing a version where Father Christmas drops a coin down the chimney, a design that carries an 1889

made bodies and were dressed in red felt or cotton fabric edged with fur, fake fur or cotton batting.

Smaller Santas, especially those intended for Christmas trees, were often made almost entirely of cotton wool, though the face was sometimes a chromo and tinsel and feathers were occasionally added. Many of these attractive figures were destined for the huge American market and are not easy to find in Britain, where Christmas was celebrated more economically. By the end of the nineteenth century, most German

patent. The Stevens Santa is a gnome-like figure, wearing a knee-length coat and a hood. Hubley, of Lancaster, Pennsylvania, made very decorative sleighs, with well-modelled reindeer, in cast iron, an atavistic material that the Americans made their own for the manufacture of toys. Some of the banks and models look nineteenth century, but were in fact still in production in the 1930s and there are many reproductions, which are not easy to recognise if the cast iron has been 'antiqued'.

Because of the cessation of German imports in the 1914-18 War, Japanese Santa Claus figures flooded into America, though the majority were of celluloid or bisque rather than metal. While the colour of these Japanese imports was unusually harsh, the designs were excellent because they were not constrained by the shadow of St. Nicholas, which discouraged too much humour and caricature. From Japan came celluloid Santas in motor cars, hanging from air balloons, swinging on Christmas bells, rolling as a Kelly on a ball-like base, or sitting in a sleigh or shoe. Obviously such fragile figures had a very short life, especially as they were likely to explode if hung on the Christmas tree near a candle, so they are now avidly collected both in Japan and America. By the 1930s, some excellent celluloid Santa figures were made in America, especially by the Irwin Company of New York and Chicago. Though celluloid dolls and toys were made in Britain by several companies, Father Christmas obviously held little appeal as a subject and the finest pieces are of Japanese or American origin.

Any antique Christmas items that carry images of Father Christmas now attract great interest, as the choice is wide enough to form a substantial collecting field. Cigarette lighters, miniature china, tree stands, buttons, tree skirts and carpets, light bulbs, printed fabric dolls, carved and glass figures are all encompassed within 'Santa collectables'. The presence of Father Christmas on a box-lid or among the pictures in a set of

With his glass icicle beard, the design of this Father Christmas has its roots in the traditional Christmas Man. Made in Germany, c.1875, the icicles make the figure very rare. Ht. 19in (48.3cm).

nursery blocks can double the value of a piece, especially if the item was manufactured before 1920.

Despite the globalisation of Christmas celebrations and the loss of folk or even national traditions, the essential morality of St. Nicholas still permeates the family festival. In Germany and Britain, Father Christmas clings more closely to his saintly origins than in America, where the boisterous, fat Santa Claus rules the season with his cry of 'Ho! Ho! Ho!'.

CHAPTER VIII
Greetings to the World

'Welcome then, old Christmas,
Friend so bright and dear
Welcome happy season
King of all the year'

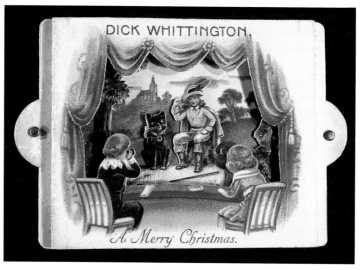

A three-dimensional card showing a scene from *Dick Whittington*.
Unmarked, c.1900.

Like most Christmas delights and traditions, attractive coloured cards with personal greetings and messages originated in Germany but were commercialised by a fortuitous combination of three factors: the penny post, an improved envelope and a more affluent public with a desire to celebrate the season of goodwill. Though the first British Christmas card appeared in 1843, it was not until the 1870s that the sending of cards became common in most families, fostered by the popularisation of the old festival through songs, carols, prints and books. By 1875, the middle-class celebration of Christmas had emerged, with a definable concern for the poor and exploited affecting national consciousness in Britain and America, largely through the work of Charles Dickens and other social reformers. This curious mixture, of selfishness and charity, plays and moves around a theme that occurs time and time again in late nineteenth century cards, which show ragged children gazing through the windows of a toy shop or a little waif with only a hungry bird or dog to keep her company in the snow.

Despite the often mawkish sentimentality of many of these designs, they did soften a few hearts and carried some concept of compassion into the lives of working people in industrial areas, whose attitudes were often

Left: The earliest type of German greetings cards carry the addition of an applied chromo. In this version, c.1870, the addition gives richness to the basic colour print.

Right: Transformation cards are the current favourites, as so few have survived in perfect working order. When the cord is pulled, the gifts are concealed within the tree. c.1870. Ht. 6in (15.2cm).

callous and hard through their own privations. Christmas cards, with their messages of goodwill, the love of God, family and friends and their gentle but persistent exposure of the state of the poor, were much more than a vehicle for greeting, as they popularised everything that complemented Christmas, from Santa, the blazing hearth, angels, robins, waits, cakes and crackers to the Nativity itself, with its hope for the world.

Shopping for family and friends became a much more social activity in the mid-nineteenth century, with a variety of specialist dealers setting up in the small towns across Europe. Instead of writing to London for dress fabrics and furniture, it was becoming possible to buy all that was required for civilised living locally. Present-giving and the sending of cards would not have become as popular without the attractive displays set out in shop windows and on the counters of general stores. In late November, all the shops in the smallest German towns

adapted their stock for Christmas with an enthusiasm that was not seen in Britain, the Netherlands or America until the last quarter of the nineteenth century. The printsellers' and stationers' windows were packed with the image of the Infant Jesus and with dozens of ornamental calendars. William Hewitt, in a book published in 1842 recalling his years spent in Germany, describes the December shops, with their

Large three-dimensional cards, such as this cat by Raphael Tuck, c.1890, always appeal. Ht. 14in (35.6cm).

'Britain's Bulwark', a perpetual calendar printed with scenes of the Napoleonic Wars and famous ships, c.1810. Hand-coloured print 16in (40.6cm) x 18in (45.7cm).

displays of cards, ornamented with coloured wreaths and with gilding and painting:

'Containing every imaginable emblem of love and friendship, hearts, doves, Cupids, flames and scrolls on which is inscribed some tender sentiment. These are intended to enclose in envelopes and as billets doux; in fact to serve the purpose of our Valentines, but the Germans do not keep Valentine's day but send such things now (i.e. Christmas) and on other occasions. These are, however, far more tasteful and beautiful than any Valentines that we have seen in England. Many of these cards have their centres cut out, leaving only a margin, like the frame of a picture, on which is a wreath of embossed flowers. The centre, or where the picture would be, is covered with a piece of white crepe, on which are fixed different coloured devices as birds, flowers etc.; or a little book, bound in mother of pearl, appears accidentally laid in the centre, which, when you lift up the cover, shows you written on it some affectionate sentence.'

Hewitt's description of the greetings cards common in Germany in the early 1840s establishes the fact that special envelopes were already available and that features which later became commonplace, such as embossed borders, cut out centres and 'books' that could be opened to reveal messages, heralded designs which were to become available in America and Britain much later.

Before 1850, most greetings were conveyed by letter but the introduction of cheap cards meant that the many people who were barely literate were able now to communicate with acquaintances or customers in an acceptable manner. In the eighteenth century, tradesmen had presented Christmas sheets and almanacs as complimentary tokens, though many were also sold cheaply to the general public by pedlars. In towns, the bellmen and the watchmen, who were employed by the people, gave these decorative seasonal woodcuts as tokens to important local figures. The 'Tree of Life' was very popular as a subject, as was the Nativity, but there were also many secular subjects,

Far right: Cards with images of Santa are very popular, especially when seen in combination with contemporary transport. This silvered postcard is dated Dec. 31, 1905. Courtesy Angela Owen

Right: Well-dressed children, from the security of their home, giving alms to a poor shivering boy in the street, would not have offended the Victorian conscience, which would have commended the gift givers. Christmas card, c.1880.

Three-dimensional cards were always expensive and were treasured by the recipients because of the lavish colours. Die-cut, c.1890. Ht. 5 ½in (14cm). *Courtesy Angela Owen*

Right: A transformation card, c.1920, in the form of a post box with letters and a postal order, which is the last piece to unfold as the cards emerge from the red box. Ht. 5 ½in (14cm). *Courtesy Angela Owen*

such as couples dancing around a Twelfth Night cake or 'Christmas Drawing Near', symbolised by an eye and a dove. Both the almanacs and the Christmas sheets have attracted collectors since the early 1900s, the range being augmented with early New Year's greetings cards. Charles Drummond, a Leith printer, published a card of this type in 1841, showing a print of a laughing man, apparently the earliest of its kind. Woodcuts were cheap to print and provided tradesmen with an ideal seasonal token they could offer as an appreciation of custom. Many of the best designs date from the 1820s and '30s and were sometimes hand coloured.

The first recorded Christmas card, with a sketch and a message of greeting, was commissioned by Sir Henry Cole in 1843. Instead of writing his usual letter of Christmas greetings, he decided to publish a coloured card with the message 'A Merry Christmas and a Happy New Year to you' written on a banner which was draped over a rail. On the lower right hand corner was a space for the sender's signature, with the

This American card carries 'Woolson Spice Co.'s Christmas Greetings' and has an 1890 copyright and 'Lion Coffee Picture card – a picture in every packet'.

132

recipient's name at the centre top. The card was designed by John Calcott Horsley and they originally cost 1/- each, a high price for the time. Very few of these cards still exist and they remain every enthusiast's dream find. They are marked 'Published at Summerley's Home Treasury Office, 12 Old Bond Street. London'. This publishing business was partly owned by Cole, though the tradition remains that the first cards were not commercial and were intended only for his friends. Perhaps because Cole was so famous, through his involvement with public affairs, including the establishment of the Royal College of Music and his association with the Great Exhibition, his cards received undue attention and there might well be others as yet unknown.

The hand-coloured Horsley card, with rustic branches twined with ivy, shows several generations of a family sitting drinking at a table. Their Christmas is obviously a very low-key affair and portrays the period

before decorated trees and elaborate table centres became common in middle-class families. The persistent message that any Christmas celebrations should be linked with charity is revealed in the Horsley card, with side panels showing a beggar receiving alms from a tray and a poor mother and her baby being wrapped in a woollen shawl for protection. Cole's concept of a greetings card was not a great imaginative leap, as a much more attractive envelope was already in existence: 'Fores's Christmas Envelope' was published in 1840 and designed by Richard Doyle. At the centre was Harlequin, ready to eat his plum pudding, surrounded by scenes of children with toys, the waits and the Punch and Judy man. It must have been a short step to design greetings cards to fit these envelopes. Improvements in colour printing techniques in the second quarter of the nineteenth century, especially Baxter's sensitively coloured small prints, which were ideal for gift boxes, scrap books and valentines,

Prints, chromos and Christmas cards were mixed together on the pages of this Victorian scrap book, c.1880. Frequently the first half of these books were tastefully arranged and the quality diminished or petered out completely before the end.

Right: Attractive Christmas catalogues were sent across the world by the larger stores. The cover of John Barker's Christmas Supplies catalogue for 1904.

  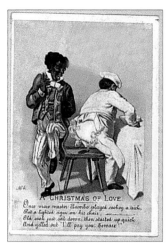 

Above: Any Christmas cards of black people are now highly collectable. 'Sambo' capering with an irate chef is from an unmarked series, c.1885.

Below: Cheap postal rates made it possible for shops to send complimentary cards to their customers. With an eye on the colonial market, William Whiteley's Department Store card for 1892. With a Porchester Terrace, London address.

encouraged stationers to set up attractive displays of cards and printed Christmas letter sheets.

In Germany, several printers were developing colour lithography and by 1830 steel embossing dies were used. Once the techniques became cheap enough, they were adapted for use in the manufacture of scraps and confectionery mottoes, which were used in particular on Christmas cakes and biscuits. The flowers, doves, Christkinder and clasped hands were printed in sheets and hand-tinted before embossing. Cutting dies speeded up production in the 1850s, the two processes eventually being combined. At this period, the subject matter of the much simpler steel engravings, sold in Britain as 'Humorous Scraps', was much more robust and provides vignettes of contemporary life which contribute more to our historical knowledge than the sentimental, but pretty, German coloured versions. The introduction of improved cutting machinery and, in 1863, the first machine-driven lithographic printing machine, meant that sheets of pre-cut, embossed scraps and pictures could be produced economically. The advances led to a deluge of colour printed publications of all kinds. Gone were the days of laborious hand-colouring and soft colours, instead every gift shop and stationer's became a tapestry of glowing colours.

Mid-nineteenth century colour printing, whether revealed in printed pictures for the home, Christmas cards, scraps or books, still astonishes because it was so labour-intensive. Sheets were passed more than twenty times through the press to achieve a richness of colour that would be totally uneconomical today. German

In scrap books, pieces cut from prints and magazines were often mixed with chromos. The best pages have a natural balance. c.1880.

Christmas card albums were a popular gift in the last quarter of the 19th century and provide a commentary on the wide variety of cards available.

printing of the 1860s is commercially unsurpassed and it is this sheer quality that lures collectors into the specialist fields of Christmas cards, scraps or gift boxes. Many of these pieces have to be assessed purely on the basis of attractiveness and quality, as they are unmarked, though most originated in the printing houses of Berlin, Leipzig and Dresden. Christmas cards frequently carry the publisher's name, as well as that of the printer, while some also reveal the signature or name of the designer.

As Christmas greetings cards became more popular, well-known artists were employed to produce illustrations that would appeal to all sections of society. The price range of Christmas cards varied widely, with silk-fringed versions originally selling for the highest figure. The cheapest were obviously the small, single sheet cards, but even these have appeal because of the fine printing. In many cards, scraps were used as a decoration on silk or embossed paper, though the confectioners remained the best customers for the chromo printers, such as Hagelberg, Nister and

Raphael Tuck, with their 'Fine Arts Works in Bavaria'.

Large chromos were often produced as a series of pictures on a related theme, such as Children's Party Games, the Ages of Man or the Life of Queen Victoria, and these remain the most expensive, especially if complete or with their original envelopes. Top quality chromos usually have the publishing details printed on each scene and exhibit state-of-the-art printing techniques. Very large Christmas chromos, though fine quality, are often completely unmarked, presumably because so many were intended for the confectionery or gift box trades. Because the scraps were so attractive, they were often lifted off biscuits and cakes and glued into the bound scrap books which were a feature of nursery life until the 1914-18 War, when German imports of the books and chromos were halted. Though later scrap books contain interesting contemporary printing and comments on social life, they never achieve the artistic elegance of those compiled in the Victorian and Edwardian periods.

Scrap books are a treasury for card and chromo

Left: 'A Kettle of Mischief', a calendar for 1901 pasted into a contemporary scrapbook.

Right: Shaped cards were a novelty in the 1880s. This round nativity scene with an angel is signed A.P. Lyton and dated 1888.

collectors, especially those that are dated and contain contemporary references. Many items of printed ephemera would be unrecorded, were it not for the enthusiasm of the compilers of scrap books, with their pages of dated cards and post cards. Other Christmas cards were glued to scrap screens, which became popular with people of average means, who were previously starved of cheap, attractive colours and designs for the home, and could not bear to discard the lovely scenes and touching messages.

In the late 1870s, steel plates were gradually replacing the old lithographic stones and contributing to a lowering of price for all printed designs. Calendars, advertisements, Christmas trade cards, box lids, book marks and writing paper all offer collecting themes, though it is the cards and chromos that are most popular, because of the vast range of designs. While embossed chromos could be used to make or enliven Christmas cards, they were superseded in the 1880s by a huge, specialist card industry that employed leading artists to introduce new images each year. The designing of Christmas cards became a useful sideline for many gifted amateur painters, who introduced a wide range of genre, humorous and novelty subjects.

All the advances of technology that made printing more economical would have had little impact on the greetings card market if postal charges had remained high. In Britain, the fee used to be paid by the recipient and could be exorbitant, depending on the distance. The introduction of the penny post in 1840 meant that letters could be sent to anyone in Great Britain at such a low cost that, between 1840 and 1845, the number of letters sent rose from 170 to 300 million. In America, reduced postal rates were introduced in 1845, though the attractive uniform rate, resembling the British penny post, was not achieved until 1883, when two cents became standard. Postcards, which did not require envelopes, were even cheaper and were first introduced in 1870. Like unsealed Christmas cards, they could be posted for ½d, so the poorest families could afford to send a few cards, while businesses were able to deluge their customers with advertising material under the guise of a goodwill message.

Queen Victoria granted a Royal Warrant to Raphael Tuck in 1893, as she sent thousands of cards to her neighbours at Windsor and Osborne, as well as other

European monarchs and her court. In 1895, she chose a Nativity scene of the Wise Men offering their gifts, a large card that opened out and stood twelve inches high by eight inches deep. Mrs Cleveland, the American First Lady, chose a simple design, described as 'almost Puritan in nature'. Large folding cards, like that chosen by Victoria, were necessarily expensive, as they were made up of so many sections, which had to be slotted, tabbed or glued together. Several designers were critical of these over-complicated designs, including a German immigrant, Louis Prang, of Roxbury, Boston, who started work as a lithographer in 1856 and, after some experimentation, began to use zinc plates from 1884. Like Sir Henry Cole, he was motivated by educational interests and believed that cheaper printing should introduce aesthetic appreciation into the lives of ordinary people. He set up competitions for card designs and organised exhibitions, both to market his cards and to increase public interest in the subject. He believed that Christmas cards should be simple, with no folding sections, lace or novelties. Good design and tasteful

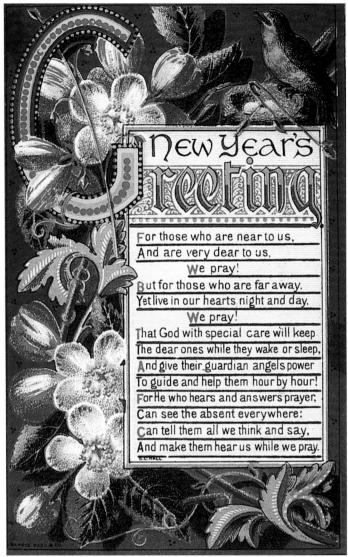

A Marcus Ward and Co. New Year's card, printed in the rich, dark colours that were popular at the end of the 19th century.

Christmas roses, with their association with the Virgin Mary, were popular on Christmas cards until the First World War. c.1880.

verses were basic to his creations, though expensive silk fringes were used on his top quality products in the 1880s. Prang cards were accepted as the pinnacle of good taste in Britain as well as America, partly because of the large number of colour passes and also because he used leading artists, whose designs were specifically created for cards, rather than being adaptations. Regrettably Prang ceased publication of Christmas

A page from a late Victorian Christmas card album, with a contrasting range of sophisticated and highly sentimental subjects.

cards in the 1890s, though other American firms, such as Albert M. Davis and Farmer, Livermore and Co. continued his tradition, though perhaps not with his vision of educating public taste.

The task of changing social attitudes was left to the writers and artists who contributed work to magazines and card publishers. As most cheap magazines relied on line drawings for their engraving workshops before the general use of photographs, there were thousands of creative people, who themselves often worked for very little and in poor conditions, to keep the presses rolling and the Christmas issues delivered. Many were all too aware of the privations of the poor from their own experience and they were not afraid of revealing the uncomfortable foundations of Victorian middle class affluence to the increasing numbers who read magazines and purchased Christmas cards.

The message and impact of the poem 'Christmas Day in the Workhouse', published in 1877, is now lost and sanitised through frequent jokes and parodies, but it was a chillingly realistic story of a poor man watching his wife die from cold and starvation and was recited at many family gatherings and local concerts. George R. Sims, the writer, also contributed a series of articles to the *Daily News* on the dreadful social conditions prevailing in London but in the poem he forced people to look at the injustices of contemporary life with such skill that the most cynical reader still sorrows for that man over a hundred years later. Dozens of similar stories and poems were contributed to many cheaply produced books and magazines which, because of the spread of literacy, were read by workers in the industrial areas, as well as by their employers, who were moved towards various phil-anthropic gestures. The Christmas card images of children begging, or lying in the snow in ragged, inadequate clothes, must have touched all but the hardest of hearts, especially when such scenes were witnessed every day in the streets of the big cities. To avoid

Left: A lace-effect celluloid card with an attractive wax-like finish. Still in its original box, cards of this type were virtually small gifts. Unmarked, c.1910. Ht. 4in (10.2cm).

Right: A three fold card of infants in the winter costumes of wealthy children.

contemporary reality, card publishers in the nineteenth century frequently resorted to idealised scenes from the past: the coaches laden with gifts and poultry, the waits carolling outside the manor house or gargantuan feasts in medieval-style halls. Bonny babies, beautiful women, kisses under the mistletoe and Father Christmas laden with gifts spread an idealised seasonal message, a message that became much stronger as the commercial aspect of the celebrations became more important.

For card enthusiasts, the richest period is between 1875 and 1910, as colour printing was still of the highest quality and many experimental and novelty ideas were being introduced. Animated, mechanical, transformations and various tableaux all competed with one another and are now among the most expensive purchases for antique card collectors. Kate Greenaway, Louis Wain, the cartoonist W. G. Baxter, Mabel Lucy Attwell and Walter Crane are among the many well known artists whose card designs are of

interest today and attract individual specialisation.

The cheerful vulgarity and heavy sentimentality of the Christmas greetings merchandise, including cards, prints and calendars, was frequently criticised in publications such as *The Studio*, the arbiter of good taste, but the tinselled Christkind, the beaded and feathered fans, the lattice-work and the silk flowers are now appreciated as typical of their period. In some card albums, with dated examples, the development of design can be traced through the centuries. Queen Mary kept albums throughout her life, a practice begun in childhood, and she included cards from other Royal families as well as home-made nursery pieces from her grand-daughter, now Queen Elizabeth II. Family card albums from all sections of society provide fascinating glimpses of life in the colonies or the armed services, as well as changes in public taste that convert the sentimentality, dated humour and national events of the Victorian period into beguiling remembrances of a Christmas past.

CHAPTER IX
A Time for Giving

'Ye who now do dress the poor
Shall yourselves find blessing'
Good King Wenceslas, Traditional carol

Any toys with a Christmas theme have special appeal. The picture blocks, with their scenes around the Christmas tree, show the variety of contemporary toys that made Christmas morning a delight. German, c.1880.

Christmas in the 1840s was felt to be a fast declining festival, with writers complaining that its olden glories were gone, in all probability never to be remembered. Many elderly people, who recalled the season in the eighteenth century, complained that the traditional revels and roistering had been abandoned in favour of holy observance, moderation and depressingly pious reflection. For a short period, the spirit of Christmas had lost its way, confused by staid Victorian morality, until it discovered a fresh role as a friend, protector and gift-bringer for children. Christmas, as it is recognised today, took its form in the last quarter of the nineteenth century, when its popularity increased, together with the growing commercial exploitation, which has always concerned those who love the festival itself but which is now so interwoven that it has helped agnostics to accept the winter celebration as happily as Christians.

The forces that were to change Christmas beyond all recognition were becoming powerful by the 1840s. British import duties on foreign foods were considerably reduced, which encouraged shops to stock sweetmeats and crystallised fruits produced in France and Spain, while the interests of poor people were served by the many goose clubs, where small amounts of money could be set aside each week for the Christmas feast. The

The Magi, who carried gifts to the infant Jesus, linked the ancient Saturnalian practice into Christian tradition. Bohemian School.

working classes across Europe and America were also becoming much better off, with good wages paid in heavy industry and some of the specialised manufacturing areas. The lure of a better standard of living impelled families to move across the world to seek a better life – one of the attractive features of working in the richer industrial areas was the freedom to celebrate Christmas without counting every small coin, as their forefathers had done.

German-style Christmases, though idealised in prints of the Royal Family, would not have held such appeal were it not for the unusually cold winters, with an extraordinary amount of snow, that were a feature of the 1830s and 40s. Scenes of people skating in fur coats and villages cut off by deep drifts transported German winters to Britain and inspired artists to portray the effect of lighted windows shining across the snow, happy families grouped around blazing log fires and children's delight as they sped down hills on sledges and toboggans. Antiquarians and researchers, by delving into country customs and publishing almost-forgotten carols and sayings, made the history of Christmas interesting, a special time, a time to draw the curtains and enjoy the better things of life within the family.

Improvements in communications, especially by the extension of the railway network across Europe, meant that, for people working in towns and cities, Christmas visits home became an affordable possibility. By the end of the century 'Home for Christmas' was becoming a reality for the working and

'Un Nöel Lorrain au Printemps', the store's Christmas toy catalogue for 1912. A procession following behind the saint is a characteristically French convention. Printed by Draeger.

Below: The snowman hat, the ultimate fashion accessory for the 1880s. German unmounted chromo.

middle classes as well as the very rich. Celebration cakes and food, trips to the pantomime, a decorated tree, rows of greetings cards and heaps of presents all marked this special occasion across the country. Few people were concerned that many rituals had developed comparatively recently and soon chose to embellish Christmas with their own family traditions. It is this continuing adaptability of Christmas that has ensured its survival, as well as the ability of institutions, shops and churches to choose certain facets for specialised development.

Many European families had relatives who had emigrated to America in the 1840s and '50s and who wrote home of the extravagance of the New York ballrooms, shops and restaurants at Christmas. By the last quarter of the nineteenth century, department stores in Manhattan were competing to stage the most eye-catching displays, with

special teams of artists and craftsmen working throughout the year on the extravagant tableaux. In America, the Christmas season begins with Thanksgiving Day, on the third Thursday in November, with rejoicing and exciting parades, such as that introduced in the 1920s by Gimbel's of Philadelphia. Sometimes live animals or big papier mâché figures were used in the parades, though in 1928 huge shaped balloons were used instead. Macey's, established in 1858, because of the importance of its toy department, has remained a Mecca for New York children looking for quality toys, while Lord and Taylor, with its windows fitted with lifts, so that scenes can be lowered into place, specialises in tableaux that attract complete families, who queue obediently to file past. The Lord and Taylor's displays are now assembled by over a hundred people working throughout the year to provide New Yorkers with an annual treat. Saks Christmas windows, created by the same team, attract similar family visits and these displays travel after their unveiling on Fifth Avenue to other stores around the country. New York has celebrated Christmas in style since the 1880s, with thousands flocking to the city to do the round of department store windows, the Angel Tree at the Metropolitan Museum and the lit tree at the Rockefeller Centre, with its tipsy aluminium angels designed by Valerie Clarebout. This huge tree is a successor to the Madison Square Park tree, first set up in 1912 when the concept of an electrically-lighted outdoor tree was itself a revelation.

European shops were never decorated with as little regard to cost as those in America. In London, Liberty's and Selfridge's competed for the most exciting windows, with Harrod's aiming at a more conservative taste. Most of the department stores published Christmas catalogues and those of Bon Marché and Galeries Lafayette in Paris are an invaluable record of contemporary styles and taste. Nineteenth century journalists enthused at the variety of gift displays in Schoolbred's, Swan and Edgar's and

N° 16   TABLEAUX AUXILIAIRES DELMAS   N° 16

A very rare Christmas shop guide for the Delmas store, c.1885, indicating where merchandise could be found by numbers. The large Christmas tree towers in the centre.
Courtesy Constance King Antiques

Below: Christmas children are often a curious amalgamation of angels and idealised, beautifully dressed winged girls. German chromo-lithographed scraps, c.1885.

Debenham and Freebody's in London, with their presents for families and servants and, above all, for children, who were beginning to rule Christmas by their demands.

Gift-giving has formed a central part of the Saturnalian festival since ancient times and in Rome the presents given during the Kalends, the first part of a month, were of the greatest importance with branches of evergreen from the grave of the goddess Strenia presented on January 1st to the glory of the Emperor. Gradually, the branches were replaced by gifts of gold or small cakes, the whole ceremony being illuminated by candles, which were lighted to symbolise eternal life. The Roman style of gift-giving was part of a ritual, though from antiquity there was a Saturnalian exchange of personal presents, with special dolls and toys for children.

By the medieval period, the giving of costly gifts among princes and nobles formed part of the ritual of statesmanship, with the most expensive pieces being put on public view. Some mid-nineteenth century Christmas presents were also surprisingly extravagant but were excused by the puritanical as 'lessening the weight of the times'. For ladies, a ball-gown or a warm winter mantle was suggested as appropriate, though in 1847 Carpenter and Westley's 'Improved Phantasmagoria Lanterns with Chromatrope and Dissolving Views' were recommended as the ideal gifts for adults, who could then stage amusing shows for all the family. Magic Lanterns rapidly became a feature of the Victorian Christmas and were supplied with specially painted greetings slides and appropriate Christmas stories, so that father could become a showman for the evening.

Bon Marché of Paris on the cover of their toy catalogue for 1922 portrayed Santa as a frisky, leaping figure, pulled to the sky by a balloon.

Wooden bonbonnières of this type appeared on the cover of a 1912 French toy catalogue, accompanied by crinolined lady versions. The Regency style man stands on the box lid. Ht. 8in (20.3cm).

In some parts of Europe, the ancient Saturnalian rituals survived into the mid-nineteenth century, with a corresponding acceptance of bad behaviour, especially on the part of young men, who shot peas at windows and knocked on doors, until they were placated with a few coins or apples. In Württemberg in Swabia, the children ended their aggressive performances with the rhyme 'Knock, knock; I'll thank ye for bread, He who don't give it, I'll break his head'. This ancient and aggressive attitude to present-giving in Swabia was accompanied by a bogey-man, who threatened children with a stick. He was obviously a close relative of Pelze-Nicol but was called 'Pelzmärte' and emerged on Christmas Eve. He had a blackened face, carried a basket and was dressed in fur. Pelzmärte has less connection with the saintly St. Nicholas than with goblins, witches and demons, always believed to be about on Christmas Eve. In some German churches, while an alarm bell tolled, crops and cattle were protected and the Father of Evil could be asked for special favours. Christmas Eve was perceived as a particularly dangerous time to be abroad, because of the number of malign presences attracted by the ancient festival. In remote parts of Europe there was a tradition that the sun took two leaps in pure joy and cattle fell on their knees as good triumphed on this special night.

The association of witchcraft and Christmas underlines the conflict between good and evil that occurs repeatedly throughout the years. In true

Bringing gifts and good cheer to the poor at Christmas was a duty that no Christian gentlewoman could shirk. George Sheridan Knowles (1863-1931).
Courtesy Christie's Images

145

Carol singing was a useful way to finance Christmas for both old and young. Drawing by Phiz, c.1845.

Opposite: A Christmas advertisement for Weldon cottons, designed and signed by Louis Wain, c.1900.

seasonal style, there are always remedies at hand and witches could be identified on Christmas Eve, though the methods of achieving this often called for considerable ingenuity. One Swabian trick was to carry a wooden ladle to church with a hole bored in the bowl. By looking through this during the sermon, any witches could be seen as they all carried milk-pails on their heads. However, if the worshippers were not safely back in their homes before the Christmas bells ceased, they

would be torn to pieces by evil spirits. Some of these ancient beliefs were perpetuated in the illustrations on nineteenth century cards and box lids, where witches and magic symbols appear among the toys and decorations, combining ancient, primitive cultures with an overlay of Christianity.

Gifts from masters to servants were presented from antiquity and could take the form of new clothes or, in the meaner households, a length of flannel or cambric that the women were expected to make up. Pepys writes of giving his servant a Christmas box and in 1711 Dean Swift gave his man Patrick 'Half a crown on condition that he be good'. In return for this, the recipient rolled home drunk at midnight.

In towns and large villages, the watchmen, bell-ringers, road-sweepers and beadles all received a gift of money from their local authorities. Servants and apprentices were happy to join in the practice of asking for donations in their earthenware boxes, which were smashed open on Boxing Day, 26 December. Though the Boxing Day tradition was peculiarly British, there were similar seasonal appeals for tips in every country celebrating Christmas.

Good deeds and gift-giving began in Victorian times with the traditions of St. Thomas' Day, the patron saint of old people. This saint's day, 21 December, had a very practical application, as elderly people received money that they could spend on Christmas food. In many parts of Britain, the poor would visit the homes of the rich to ask for alms, a custom known as 'going a-gooding'. Clergymen were favoured as targets, as the church could hardly refuse help, though anyone with money was fair game for local children, with their song 'Christmas is coming, the goose is getting fat. Please to put a penny in the old man's hat'. Both the elderly, who went 'mumping' or 'going a-gooding' and the children with their songs gave a sprig of holly in return for gifts of money. Many of the adults were so regaled with spiced ale in the kitchens of large houses that

Musical boxes decorated with applied paper scenes of Father Christmas or snowmen made appealing gifts. Made by Thorens of Switzerland, c.1910. The movement can be wound in either direction. Marked 'Swiss D. Des. 70999-71905'. 2¾in (7cm) diameter.

Left: Struwwelpeter was the most popular German children's gift book in the mid-19th century, as its moral tales appealed to adults. *The English Struwwelpeter* was published by Griffith, Farran, Okeden and Welsh.

their journeys home were long and hazardous. In other parts of Britain, Advent Images, a pre-Reformation custom, were carried around local houses by Image Bearers. These figures represented Jesus and the Virgin Mary and their display was accompanied by the singing of a special carol. If the Image Bearers forgot to call at a particular house, then bad luck was foretold.

Threats of ill fortune and visits by witches were forgotten in all but the most remote areas by 1850, when giving was more influenced by the ideals of the church and philanthropists, who believed in helping the deserving poor. Christmas treats were anticipated by the poor throughout the year and were organised by the owners of great estates, churches, the Salvation Army and various charitable organisations. Money was raised for the Treat by summer fetes and bazaars and the gifts were given to every person, young or old,

who was known to be poor. Usually the presents received were in the form of tickets for coal or blankets that could be redeemed in local shops.

A writer in *The Lady* in 1906 described how the organiser of a treat had written 'Welcome' on a long strip of white calico, with festoons of red, white and blue muslin as a border. There were flags, Chinese lanterns and holly massed with berries and, in advice to organisers of similar events, she stated: 'Let there be no stint in the size of fires and the number of gas jets or lamps, light and warmth being the greatest luxuries for old folk.' Just in case they should enjoy themselves too much, 'Intoxicants are better avoided, with the exception of a hot glass of elder wine, to be served at the end of the repast to each loyal subject, while the King's health has to be drunk and the pianist plays the National Anthem as loud as she can'.

The menu for the Christmas Treat was equally cautious: bread and butter, hot strong tea, cake, cold roast beef and hot Christmas pudding, served 'in a blaze of fire'. After the tables were cleared, there were toasts before the distribution of presents, mainly shawls, socks, petticoats and scarves. Then the men could light their pipes and gifts of tobacco were sent round, while songs like 'Sally in our Alley' and 'Home, Sweet Home' were sung. For the children's party, there were plain teas, then presents from the Christmas tree and a bag of buns and oranges to take home. It was essential that the Christmas tree should be screened off and the candles lit at the very last minute, as they did not last very long and it was dangerous to allow them to burn too low. Often, a large bucket of water stood behind the tree with a long handled mop, so that any threatening conflagration could be doused.

There was little problem with finding pianists for Christmas Treats or family gatherings, as learning to play an instrument was thought to be an essential part of a child's education. Cheap pianos stood in the front rooms of cottages in industrial areas, as well as middle-class homes, and were in regular use for sing-songs and concerts. This market, which grew steadily until the Second World War, was supplied by a vast music publishing industry, which brought out new albums and Christmas sheets each year. Some of the covers are so attractive that they now form a specialist collecting area, as do the albums, with their many illustrations and leather-bound cases. Books and carol sheets often showed prints of waits singing under a lantern and invariably dressed in eighteenth century style. Originally, waits were employed as watchmen or minstrels who guarded the streets and called the hours, though by the late nineteenth century, most town waits had become musicians, who played wind

In this bonbonnière, the upper body lifts to reveal the container. The boy on a sledge has a bisque head made by Gebrüder Heubach, c.1910. Some gift boxes were so complex that they formed attractive toys in their own right. Ht. 5 ½in (14cm).

Wax-headed bonbonnière dolls are uncommon. This girl, carrying a gift of flowers, is dressed in cotton batting with mica decoration. The whole body is a cylindrical box lid. She has glass eyes and wax arms. German, c.1880. Ht. 7 ½in (19cm).

instruments in return for donations. The origin of the waits is not known but they took their place among Nativity scenes, medieval feasts and family gatherings illustrated so lavishly on the music covers.

'Good King Wenceslas' is one of the most popular carols, especially with children, who often confuse him with St. Nicholas himself. Wenceslas was born in the tenth century in what is now the Czech Republic, and became a Christian under the tuition of priests who were smuggled into his home. He was established as a brave leader when he defeated an attempt to take over his country by the Duke of Bavaria. Astonishingly, he was only thirteen when he achieved this and five years later he had become the Christian leader of Bohemia. A mythology of story and legend developed around the young man, who freed slaves and commuted death sentences. His death at the early age of twenty-two gave him the status of a martyr, as he was murdered by his pagan brother, despite a brave attempt to save him by his page Podiven, who was later hanged. Like many Christmas stories, the words of the carol have travelled far from the story of young Wenceslas, and on the music covers we see an old, saintly figure advising his page, rather than an energetic young ruler, who did not

By the 1870s, Christmas card designers had achieved elegance, combined with Victorian sentimentality.

comply with the words of the carol so well. Instead, Wenceslas changed his form into the ancient character of 'Winter' or the 'Christmas Man', who exists in some form in all cultures.

Children confuse Wenceslas and St. Nicholas because of their long monk's robes, a costume adopted by fathers in the late nineteenth century, who crept into bedrooms in disguise to fill stockings late at night. Santa outfits were first sold in America and were appearing in British catalogues by 1900. The red coats were usually made of cheap plush or cotton and there were hats with a sprig of holly. In the most expensive Father Christmas outfits, there were wigs, beards, eyebrows, stockinet masks and several different noses. For little girls there were fairy dresses, while boys could be soldiers. Dressing up, the wearing of disguises and masks were, of course, all part of the ancient Saturnalian tradition. Once the big department stores entered into the celebration of Christmas, they organised pageants and masquerades and arranged Santa grottoes. In America, Macey's, Lichtenstein and Sons and Wanamakers on Broadway competed for the most impressive displays. In 1919, Wanamakers held a Santa parade of Eskimos, a brass band and children dressed as elves and snowflakes. Wanamakers was also

French manufacturers created the most extravagant and ephemeral gift boxes. Made of gilt paper, scraps and card, the appearance of an ivory casket was achieved, c.1870. 5 ½in (14cm) x 3 ½in (8.9cm).

A MERRY CHRISTMAS AND A HAPPY NEW YEAR.

Left: Laden with attractive gifts and ringing her Christmas bell, this child in a German chromo, c.1880, reveals the 'giving' image of the season. Ht. 6in (15.2cm).

Far left: The poor chimney-sweep seeking work in the snow, but wishing all a Merry Christmas. Card from a Victorian album.

the first to use an in-store telephone so children could ring Santa Claus.

Christmas became the true Saturnalia of children in the second half of the nineteenth century. Before this time, though a few gifts and toys were received, the celebrations, mainly feasting, were primarily intended for adults. Victoria and Albert, with their ever-growing brood of young children, demonstrated family life at its best, an image that, after the 1860s, was spread across the world in hundreds of photographs, many showing the Royal infants with their toys. Instead of keeping his children out of sight like most wealthy men of the time, Albert enjoyed their company and devised games, gardens and a little Swiss cottage for their pleasure and entertainment. Each year the most exciting event was the the celebration of Christmas in the German manner of his childhood.

Even by the mid-nineteenth century, writers were complaining that children were becoming masters of the season, with the domestic ship 'seized by a crew of mutinous little hands and navigated gaily through the frozen regions of the winter solstice with youth at the prow and pleasure at the helm'. The 1853 writer in 'Christmas Games for Evening Parties' describes the food children liked as "the wild region of flummery, with tartlets, syllabubs and whipped cream". The games suggested for family parties were The Prussian Soldier, The Health of Cardinal Puff, The Learned Pig and the Cock and Bull Story. Old favourites, like Spillikins, conundrums, tombola and snapdragon were played by everybody, as were consequences, but it is the juvenile games, especially those in attractive boxes that are now most eagerly collected.

Once lithographic colour printing was introduced, it became economic to produce games for special events and more Christmas covers are found. Puzzle blocks, jigsaws, round games and paper dolls were all issued for Christmas and now command prices completely out of line with similar toys without the Christmas connection. By the end of the century, there were musical boxes, painting, writing and sewing sets, as well as zithers and drums, all decorated with Christmas trees and Santa Claus. Kellys, balls, jumping jacks, Santa dolls and sheets of scraps were ideal for Christmas stockings, usually an old sock with a traditional piece of lucky coal in the toe. In poor families, children received an orange, a bag of nuts, some confectionery and, if they were lucky, a single toy. Every family develops its own ritual for Christmas stockings and their contents, though many now choose to substitute a capacious printed sack or an old pillow case to hold the extravagant gifts that modern children receive. All these traditions developed from the story of St. Nicholas, who gave gold as dowries to the three daughters of a man who had lost all his money. In one version, the women would have been forced into prostitution if Nicholas had not filled their stockings with gold. In Holland and France, shoes were used instead of stockings, though both traditions share a root in the legend of St. Nicholas.

Commercially made, printed fabric stockings were first produced in America and are now rare, as they

The gift box industry employed thousands of low paid workers in cities, who utilised scraps, prints, gilt lace papers and ribbons to create the most ephemeral pieces. The small box contained Fry's Cocoa, while the silk-effect box held a perfume bottle.

La Befana is fated to travel the world searching for the Christ Child because she was too busy sweeping to help the Magi. This doll has a papier mâché head and a fabric and composition body. Made in the Sonneberg region of Germany, c.1880. Ht. 11½in (29.2cm).

soon tore or became discoloured. Sometimes they featured a printed greeting or some words from a Christmas rhyme, such as 'Hang up the Baby's stocking, Be sure you don't forget'. The fabric was usually covered with scenes of children in bed, with their stockings hanging by the fire, Santa flying through the air, or elves delivering gifts and decorating fir trees. Once the Teddy Bear was introduced in 1903, he frequently appeared in the design. The styles of the toys illustrated are the best means of dating, as some of these lithographed stockings have a worn and ancient appearance which is deceptive. Paper stockings were decorated with similar prints, though few have survived, as they were functioning as a gift packet. Japanese manufactures favoured net stockings, trimmed with crepe paper, as they were so cheap and were often sold ready-filled with toys, particularly the celluloid figures always associated with Japan. Net stockings vary in size, from two to thirty-six inches long, and are often edged with crepe paper. Father Christmas figures frequently carry the smallest net Christmas stockings filled with miniature toys.

March Bothers in the USA in 1911 were selling net stockings, described as 'an exceptionally new and unique way of holding candy'. Their stockings were tied with a cord at the top and were sold complete with a presentation card. Commercially made stockings appeared on the market around 1890, the lithographed versions being much more popular in America than in Europe. Girls' and women's magazines before this date do not include patterns for making fabric Christmas stockings at home and we have to conclude that old socks or thick stockings were used. In large English country houses, thick knit shooting stockings were favourites on Christmas Eve, though in early photographs ladies' coloured stockings, which looked more attractive, are often shown hanging at the end of the bed or from the mantelpiece.

Father Christmas' use of the chimney as a means of entering and leaving the home reveals the persistence of ancient beliefs in hearth worship, with the associated veneration of the Yule log and the fear of

Made of felt-covered carton, the well-modelled dog with glass eyes comes apart at the collar to reveal a cylindrical candy container, c.1905. Ht. 6in (15.2cm).

The Guardian Angel appears in all guises on pre-1914 cards and gift boxes. This velvet covered box has a photographic print of an angel behind the glass. Made in France, c.1905, the box originally contained confectionery. 5 ½in (14cm) square.

witches, who are also abroad on Christmas Eve. Some children leave a present for Santa or place a glass of liquor on the hearth, once again harking back to beliefs shrouded in the mists of time. In Sweden, elves clamber down the chimney and through the windows by the dozen to bring gifts and are known as 'Julklapp'. In Italy, the witch-like figure Befana, derived from Epiphania, also creeps into houses down the chimney and carries a broomstick. La Befana is a sad figure, who wanders the world looking for the Christ Child. She was stopped outside her cottage by the Wise Men, who asked her to show them the way to Bethlehem. She ignored their request and went on sweeping, refusing even to give them a gift to take to the Baby. Feeling remorseful after their departure, she found a ball, a rag doll, a bunch of herbs and a fragment of purple cloth that she could have given the baby so, taking her poor gifts, she left her house and began her wandering search for the Magi and the Infant Jesus. On 5 January, Epiphany Eve, she leaves gifts for good children and sticks and stones for those that have been bad. La Befana is represented as a witch-like doll, who always carries a broom. Those dating to before 1920 having papier mâché shoulder heads and cheap fabric bodies. Sometimes the same figure is found costumed as a witch, an old Welsh woman or La Befana, but all were made in the Sonneberg factories. In some versions of the story it was the shepherds rather than the Magi who told her of the Nativity.

Today, the gift boxes themselves, rather than the items they contained appeal to collectors. The most expensive were the rabbit skin covered bonbonnières, which were so cleverly modelled in carton that they seem like live rabbits, cats and dogs of all breeds. In most instances, the head lifts off to reveal a cylindrical, cardboard-lined container for gifts, but sometimes entry is through the base or a lifting panel on the animal's back. Such bonbonnières were expensive, as makers used realistic glass eyes and it took some skill to shape the fur, felt or plush over the detailed animal forms. The most complex and realistic were made in France, where there was a large cartonnière industry, producing all kinds of gift boxes and cornucopia, which were ideal for hanging on a large Christmas tree.

American collectors can choose from an extensive assortment of candy boxes and containers, made of card and carton, which were decorated with cotton wool batting, tinsel, scraps and mica. Because the American market had become the most important in the world by 1900, they received the most progressive and innovative designs, with motor cars, aeroplanes and fire stations sold alongside traditional snow-covered churches, cottages and Alpine chalets.

Reindeer pulling sleighs, toboggans, angels with baskets and Santa with his sack are all represented in china Christmas ornaments and bonbonnières. German factories from the last quarter of the nineteenth century were producing vast numbers of cheap bisque figures especially for the seasonal market. Chocolate and candy makers were among their best customers, as the pieces could be used as table gifts for parties. Gebrüder Heubach produced a range of containers on the theme of Christmas, with children in snow-suits and polar bears pulling an empty cart. Snowballs, Father Christmas heads and sledges, logs and children in winter sports outfits standing by baskets appeared in china shops and confectioners and were popular from the 1880s, as the containers could be re-used.

The first commercially made gift containers were the cosques, cone-shaped packets, that could be hung from a tree and were decorated with tinsel, scraps, feathers or silk flowers. During the 1870s, more adventurous designs appeared such as flock or skin-covered animals, the heads forming the lids, and a myriad of beautifully ornamented boxes, intended for the luxury goods market. Most were produced in the small, garret workshops that were common to cities across the world, though the most inventive, if not the best made, work originated in France. German makers specialised in cheap, novelty items in papier mâché that rely for their effectiveness on the basic model rather than the expensive, time-consuming decoration favoured by the French. Few boxes or bonbonnières were ever marked, other than with the country of origin and they are valued by collectors for their design and rarity, rather than attribution.

Large clockwork display Santas are similarly unattributable though occasionally the mechanism provides a clue as to the country of origin. The large nodding Santas are usually sold by antique dealers as shop display items, as are the reindeer pulling sleighs, though in the old toy catalogues both are included in the pages of items intended for the home, where they were suggested as suitable for a sideboard or to place under a tree. Santa's sleigh could be filled with crackers, wrapped sweets, chocolates or a bottle of perfume:

occasionally they have an advertising slogan on the side, which adds greatly to their appeal for collectors. In America, lithographed paper was applied to wooden outline-cut sleighs, so that a very cheaply produced container could be colourful and detailed with prints of toys, dolls and, of course, Santa himself.

China and pressed glass candy containers were common after 1890, when untinted white bisque, transfer printed porcelain and, especially in America, pressed glass in novelty designs all competed for the confectionery market. Because many of these containers were of good quality, they were preserved from year to year or put in the family china cabinet. Snowmen, Santa boots, wall plaques and Santa jugs and teapots all appeal to collectors of Christmas, even those made in the 1950s are now developing a following.

It is not surprising that the collecting of Christmas-associated antiques first developed in America. In the twentieth century, celebrations of the festival have become so extravagant and accompanied by so many accessories that the old European rituals seem quiet in comparison. Once British people had begun to experience Hollywood-style American Christmases through the cinema, more glamour was introduced into their own celebrations, with more lavishly decorated houses, the imported custom of hanging wreaths on doors and the use of coloured lights to create outdoor Christmas trees. Vast piles of presents, all beautifully wrapped, were reserved for the richest people in Europe before 1955 but now, because of films and television, can be found in any home.

The American Christmas is a mixture of the more attractive elements of several European countries but one feature never accepted from Britain is the Christmas cake, with its rock-hard icing over a rich, pudding-like mixture of fruit, spices, spirits and nuts. These celebration cakes were the pride of British cooks, with some of the most spectacular creations produced in Queen Victoria's household. Though

With large round eyes, the felt-covered carton dog bonbonnière has a head that lifts off, the join neatened by the collar. c.1925. Ht. 4in (10.2cm).

America spurns iced fruit cake, the Europeans have accepted one purely American creation with delight. Rudolf the Red Nosed Reindeer, with his message that the ugliest animals can find favour with Santa Claus, instantly appealed to children and led to a boom in reindeer-related products. 'Rudolf! the Red Nosed Reindeer' was written in 1939 as a promotional poem for a mail order firm and was re-published in 1946. In 1949, with the words set to music and a host of attractive images, Rudolf became a star. He was created by Robert L. May, who worked for Montgomery Ward and is the only truly international Christmas character to have been created in the twentieth century. The song is so popular that it is sung, almost like a carol, at children's Christmas parties and concerts and almost everyone remembers yelling it at a pantomime. Like so many elements of Christmas, Rudolf has become truly international and is typically twentieth century, as he embodies the concept of the poor fellow, who can do well, and reveals the saint's concern for animals, which arouses the interest of children. Today, early Rudolf items are eagerly hunted by Christmas enthusiasts, as they can still be discovered in car boot sales and house auctions.

It is no coincidence that the collecting of Christmas-associated antiques first developed in America, a country never ravaged by war, so that old decorations were saved and passed on to children and grandchildren. Many of the finest glass ornaments and Dresdens were originally sold to this big, growing market before the First World War and it is now easier to find tree ornaments in America than in Britain or France. There are few Christmas antiques dealers in Britain, though postcards, toys and automata can all be found within these specialities, but as collectors turn their attention to pieces made in the 1950s and '60s, the possibilities of finding interesting items in general antiques shops becomes greater. Some of the leading auction rooms now have 'Christmas' sections

Children and dogs are popular on cards, especially when the breeds themselves are collectable. This Art Nouveau example folds so it can stand. Pug is tucked into a a doll's cradle for the night. c.1905
Courtesy Jane Vandell Associates

in their winter sales, where Victorian and Edwardian items are offered to serious collectors.

As in any field of antique collecting, condition is extremely important, especially in relation to ceramic pieces. Papier mâché and carton-type containers are invariably fragile and some imperfections have to be accepted, as with wax fairy dolls made before 1850, but once the areas of glass tree ornaments, chromos, cards and music covers are approached, the criteria of assessing damage become very much stricter and near perfection is required by the most committed.

There is no accepted price structure for Christmas antiques, as there is for blue and white earthenware or miniature silver, and the amounts asked by dealers for fairy dolls or gift boxes varies tremendously, suggesting that personal preference rather than any logic governs value. Obviously, the most expensive Christmas Collectables are the cast-iron and tinplate Santas in sleighs, which have climbed the heights in toy sales for

These fibrous type containers, c.1940, were made in Scotland from the 1930s. Other versions for sweets included cats, policemen and soldiers. Manufacture seems to have stopped around 1950. Ht. 8in (20.3cm).
Courtesy Constance King Antiques

The splendid black king, Balthasar, wears a much more extravagant costume than Melchior and Kaspar, who kneel with their gifts at the Infant's feet. Jakob C. Cornelisz van Amsterdam (1470-1533).

Composition shoulder-headed bonbonnière with a loofah covered body and hat. The upper section of the costume lifts off at hip level for access to the cylindrical container. German, c.1885. Ht. 11in (27.9cm).

bought, if the price is low enough, by doll collectors, who enjoy re-costuming them.

In recent years, glass tree lights have become popular, with many collectors buying individual pieces as well as complete sets. These lights include cartoon characters, Santas, Christmas houses, dolls, butterflies, flowers and stars and are now emerging as a specialist area. Since the first appearance of albums, Christmas cards have appealed to our collecting instincts, with fine condition mechanical pieces now selling in Britain for over £100. Some people specialise in Santa cards or those with toys, dolls or Christmas trees, as the variety produced is almost unending. Today the nostalgia for our own childhood motivates many collectors, who look for plastic Rudolfs or 1960s mini-skirted fairy dolls with their hair in 'flick-ups'. Because the field is so wide and there are so many possibilities of finding interesting pieces, Christmas collectors are constantly searching and discovering, always widening their knowledge and increasing their displays. Some collectors allow their acquisitions to spread over their complete home, others confine their glass decorations to a small case and others hide away their early cards and examine them as an annual treat. No matter whether valuable or fun-items are collected, every enthusiast has to be committed to the celebration of Christmas itself, that unsurpassed festival of winter.

Essentially, Christmas is a time for nostalgia, a time for meeting old friends, for visiting, trips to the theatre or the pantomime, eating exciting food and indulging our loved ones, especially children. It has survived the criticism of churches and agnostics, the cynicism and apathy of the twentieth century, yet is ever more widely celebrated, even by people who neither understand nor subscribe to its basic message. Since the ancient civilisations, humanity has needed hope in the darkness of winter and belief in spiritual forces that can soften hard hearts, bring colour into tired lives and turn ordinary people into joyful emissaries of Christmas.

decades, though the display and mechanical figures follow a close second. Any figures of Father Christmas, if made before 1939, are of interest, as are decorated artificial trees and good quality bonbonnières, while in comparison, glass tree decorations of the simplest types can be bought cheaply. Because the antiques of Christmas have such a wide price structure, they appeal both to those who enjoy cheap, but amusing, items and those who like exclusivity. Early Christmas-related antiques, such as crèche figures, paintings, samplers and sculpture, obviously fall into the realm of good general antiques and are valued accordingly. Crèche figures, which are sold as works of art, have a large following that seems to prefers the taller, more impressive figures. In general, those with the original costumes still in good condition sell for high prices, while any that are completely re-dressed or re-painted are not liked by antique specialists, though they are

Bibliography

Anon, *Krippen*, Bayerisches Nationalmuseum,1972

Anon, *Krippen*, Südwest Verlag 1970

Anon, Oberammergau Passion Play and Museum, Community of Oberammergau 1963

Anon, *Volkskunst im Diozesanmuseum Freising*, Diozesan Museum Freising, 1978

Anthology, *Christmas around the World*, New Orchard, 1985

Baker M, *Christmas Customs and Folklore*, Shire Books, 1972

Bamm P, *The Kingdoms of Christ*, Thames & Hudson, 1959

Best G, *The Home of Santa Claus*, Fisher, Unwin, 1900

Blair A, *Christmas Cards for the Collector*, Batsford, 1986

Brauneck M, *Religiöse Volkskunst*, Dümont, 1979

Brenner R, *Christmas Past*, Schiffer, 1985

Brett, *Twelve Days of Christmas*, Beehive, 1987

Buday G, *History of the Christmas Card*, Spring Books, 1964

Burnham S, *A Book of Angels*, Valentine, 1990

Campbell R J, *The Story of Christmas*, Collins undated

Cantacuzino M, *A London Christmas*, Sutton, 1989

Cooper M, *Crèche Figures*, Doll Library, 1969

Cuisenier J, *French Folk Art*, Kodansha International, 1977

Dickens C, *A Christmas Tree*, Paper Tiger, 1988

Döderlein W, *Krippengeschichten*, Pfeiffer, 1963

Flick P, *Christmas Cats*, Diamond Books, 1990

Fox H E, *Christmas time in Many a Clime*, Church Missionary Society, 1905

Frys, Iracka and Popropek, *Folk art in Poland*, Arkady, 1988

Goepfert G, Editor, *Alpenlandische Weihnacht*, Süddeutsher Verlag, 1970

Hadfield M & J, *Twelve Days of Christmas*, Cassel, 1961

Hart, Grossman and Dunhill, *Joy to the World*, Ebury Press ,1990

Hewitt W, *Rural and Domestic Life of Germany*, Longman, Brown Green and Longmans, 1842

Howard, Pool, Erwitt, *The Angel Tree*, Abrams, 1993

Just and Karpinksi, *Sächsische Volkskunst*, Seeman Verlag, 1982

Mayhew H, *German Life and Manners*, Wm. H. Allen, 1865

Miall A & P, *Victorian Christmas Book*, Dent, 1978

Morris, Desmond, *Christmas Watching*, Jonathon Cape, 1992

Morrison M, *Snow Babies, Santas and Elves*, Schiffer, 1993

Muir F & J, *A Treasury of Christmas*, Robson Books, 1991

Nettel, *Santa Claus*, Gordon Fraser, 1957

Neuhardt J & Hofstetter K, *Wachsgebild*, Pannonia, 1979

Owen T M, *Welsh Folk Customs*, National Museum of Wales, 1978

Pool Daniel, *Christmas in New York*, Seven Stories, 1997

Ringler J, *Alte Tiroler Weihnachtskrippen*, Wagner, 1969

Rogers and Hallinan, *The Santa Claus Picture Book*, Dutton, 1984

Roth E, *Ein Kind ist uns Geboren*, Prestel, 1971

Sansom W, *Christmas*, Weidenfeld and Nicholson, 1968

Schiffer M, *Christmas Ornaments*, Schiffer, 1984; *Holidays, Toys and Decorations*, Schiffer, 1985

Schleich E & E, *Frommer Sinn und Lieblichkeit*, Verlag Passavia, 1973

Smith L & D, *Christmas Collectibles*, Apple, 1993

Stille E & Pfistmeister U, *Christbaumschmuck*, Hans Carl Nürnberg, 1979

Thomas Leslie, *Midnight Clear*, Arlington, 1978

Weightman and Humphries, *Christmas Past*, Sedgwick & Jackson, 1987

Index